CRIMES & CHAOS

Avram Davidson

COPYRIGHT

Trade Paperback ISBN: 978-1-955676-08-3
EBook ISBN: 978-1-955676-09-0
Second edition paperback published 2021.
First edition paperback published 1962, Regency Book

Published by Or All The Seas With Oysters Publishing San Francisco, CA

Or All The Seas With Oysters Publishing LLC eBook Edition 2021
Or All The Seas With Oysters Publishing LLC Trade Paperback Edition 2021 Printed in the USA

www.avramdavidson.com

Chapters of this book originally appeared as magazine pieces and have been specially revised by the author for inclusion here.

THE FURNITURE FELLOW, copyright 1959 by
Fawcett Publications, Inc., as "King of the U.S.A."

THE DEATH OF THE HENRY CLAY, copyright 1959 by
Fawcett Publications, Inc., as "Death Duel of the River Kings"

MIDWIFE TO MURDER, copyright 1960 by
Fawcett Publications, Inc., as "The Riddle of Jack The Ripper"

LITTLE RENÉ, copyright 1959 by

DEDICATION

To My Wife, My Mother,

And My Child

INTRODUCTION

Welcome to *Or All the Seas with Oysters Publishing*, where you are about to embark upon a voyage into *The Avram Davidson Universe*. Within this Universe, you will find the works of Hugo, Edgar, and World Fantasy Award-winning and genre-transcending Avram Davidson, who is considered one of the finest authors of the 20th century, and the works of Grania Davis, Avram's onetime life partner and frequent writing collaborator, a dedicated preservationist of Avram's works, and a talented and acclaimed author in her own right. *Or All the Seas with Oysters Publishing* is dedicated to bringing both the out-of-print and the never-before published writings of both Avram and Grania back to life in print, audio, and e-book formats, and we look forward to making this treasured legacy accessible once again to readers, ranging from longtime fans and scholars to those just beginning this journey.

Avram's Universe is calling—we invite you to step inside.
avramdavidson.com/join-the-fan-club/

PREFACE

IT BEGINS WITH A LITTLE THING—

A military order written in ill-chosen words . . .
A puff of smoke that might be just harmless steam . . .
A scar-faced young fellow applying for a job as a speakeasy
bouncer . . .
A distant tinkle of window glass . . .

A FRIGHTENED MAN BEGINS TO RUN—A NERVOUS WOMAN
SCREAMS

A safety catch clicks . . .
A razor blade winks bright as moonbeams and slashes down-
ward out of sight . . .
MANY PEOPLE WILL DIE

A RAIN OF
BURNING GIRLS

T
HE FIRST ANYONE outside the factory knew about it was when a pane of glass came crashing into Washington Place. A horse, hitched to a wagon in the street, ran away with a whinny of fright. A man named Cardiane pressed his hat down on his head and darted across the street, shoulders hunched. He almost bumped into James Cooper, a reporter for the New York *World*, whose accidental presence in the narrow street that beautiful spring afternoon was to provide him with the story of his career.

The two men looked to see where the glass had fallen from. They scanned the two 10-story buildings occupying the block to Greene Street. The New York University Law School building showed nothing. Neither, for a moment, did the adjacent Asch Building. Then Cardiane clutched the reporter and pointed upward. From one of the Asch Building's topmost floors came a small puff of white smoke. The sign on that floor carried a name which all the world would know before midnight: TRIANGLE SHIRT-WAIST COMPANY.

Triangle was an outfit doing a million-dollar business. Its proprietors, Blanck and Harris, were known in the trade as "The Shirt-waist Kings." Union organizers called them something less kind. Their company operated three factories in New York City, of which this was the largest. It occupied the eighth, ninth, and tenth stories of the Asch Building. Here worked over 600 of the firm's 900 employees, mostly women. March 25, 1911, was a

Saturday and, although many of the help were Jewish and from sundown Friday to sundown Saturday is the Jewish Sabbath, only 50 of them had stayed home. Poverty, and the assimilating effects of an American environment, had brought the rest to work.

The great garment workers' strike of the previous year had seen some gains made by the cloak makers' union, but the waist (or blouse) makers had lost out. Among their defeated proposals were half a day's work on Saturday and more and better factory fire escapes. Those working in the Asch Building, however, were not particularly worried about this last item, for the Asch Building was fireproof. It *couldn't* be burned. It was unburnable.

Across the ocean, a great British shipyard was working on a new ship. It was to be, like the Asch Building, the last word in modern and scientific design. Not only would it be unburnable, it would be unsinkable as well. Its name was the *Titanic*.

Back orders, unfilled because of the strike, as well as new orders for the spring and summer trade made the Triangle shop hum. But it was no sweatshop, no tenement hole where people toiled till 9 at night by gaslight. Triangle was a modern, up-to-date outfit in a new building, and work would come to a halt for the day at a quarter to 5.

Some of those at work were undoubtedly unhappy because of the union's defeat, but many others were very happy, and for better reasons than that the week's labor was drawing to a close. Pauline Levine, for instance, was planning to arrange about her trousseau that night. In a month's time, she intended to quit and marry Henry Marks. She already had $50 in the bank. (Her fellow-worker, Mrs. Julia Rosen, on the other hand, didn't trust banks: they could fail and lose your money. So she kept her life savings, $857, pinned to her underwear. It was found on her body that night.)

Clothilde Terranova was also going to be married soon. So was Joseph Wilson. His fiancee, Rose Salomon, had only last night given him a ring and a watch with her picture inside the case. Joe checked the time. It was 4:40.

On the main floor at the Washington Place side of the building the operators of the passenger elevators, Frank Zito and Gaspar Mortillaro, stood by their cages. They were waiting for the signal to start for the three upper floors—the only ones where people were still at work—as soon as the Triangle factory let out. The men at the freight elevators on the Greene Street side of the building were waiting too. Both sets of lifts were used to convey people at opening and closing time. The freight elevators were much larger than the passenger ones. They were also much slower.

Cutting and sewing were done on the eighth and ninth floors, where about 200 and 300 people, respectively, were at work. On the tenth, or top, floor, which housed the pressing and designing sections as well as the offices, there were about 60 more. Diana Lifschitz, the bookkeeper, was "talking" to a girl on the tenth floor via the telautograph machine. Max Blanck, one of the owners, was in the sample room, settling an argument about some lace. His partner, Harris, was busy in the shop. In the office were Blanck's two small daughters and their governess. Samuel Bernstein, the cutting-room superintendent, was supervising the laying-out of material for future work with Max Rothen, a cutter. And Louis Brown, one of the firm's four machinists, patrolled the banks of sewing machines to see if everything was in order.

Because of the heavy workloads they carried, the machines had to be oiled frequently. And sometimes they "sparked."

Several of the men employees already had cigarettes in their mouths and had placed wooden matches behind their ears, waiting for the chance to get out and light up. To be sure, smoking inside the shop was not unknown, although it was strictly illegal and officially forbidden by the management. But some did it, anyway—cupping the cigarettes in their hands and blowing the smoke down their coat sleeves. After all—the building *was* fireproof.

The *World* (for which James Cooper, then idly strolling

through Washington Square, a few blocks away, was a reporter) carried a mixed bag of news that March 25, 1911. *Workman's Compensation Act Found Unconstitutional* read one headline. If anyone was injured at work—say in the Triangle shirt-waist factory—that was the worker's tough luck. *Blind Hymn Writer Is Happy At 97* was another story. President Taft had pink eye. The Mexican Cabinet had resigned in a body. An editorial asked a question posed before and since: "Is it possible that not one man can be found . . . in N.Y.C. to handle the police as it should be handled?"

And a college professor in Philadelphia asked a women's group: "What are you going to do with your freedom and your right to vote when you get it? Back in the beginning of the world, women were slaves . . . But now women have become social parasites . . . Man bears the burden . . . woman gets the fun . . ."

Obviously, the professor had never worked in a shirt-waist factory.

The *World* advertised Royal Bengal Cigars at 10 for 15 cents and men's madras shirts ($2 value) for $1. And Wanamaker's offered "FINE WAISTS—Chiffon and Foulard Blouses, at $3.85, $5.75, and $6.75 . . . High and low necks, all with kimono sleeves . . ."

What were physical conditions like in the Triangle plant so high above the street? Very much as in any "loft building" of the sort springing up all over lower Manhattan from Canal Street to 42nd. The Asch structure was built of stone and steel, with large windows and high ceilings. Originally, the lofts—one large room to each floor—had been intended for warehouse and sales or display purposes only. But more and more factories were moving into them. The increased access to daylight cut down on gas and electric bills. Also, New York State laws required 225 cubic feet of air for each worker. It made no difference to the State in which direction this was measured. The higher the ceilings, the closer you could cram employees.

In the Triangle shop, on the eighth and ninth floors, the sewing machines were jammed so closely together that the chairs of the girls dovetailed back to back. This was perfectly legal.

Loft buildings had no interior walls, so wooden partitions were set up, creating a series of alleys and passageways. The lanes leading to the exits were jammed with wooden and cardboard boxes and crates and pine shelves loaded with cloth, lace, and paper. Wooden worktables ran the length of the rooms, with little aisle-space at each end. The tables were covered with cloth, finished and semi-finished. Some of the finished garments lay in the wicker baskets beside each sewing machine. Others were hung overhead on wires or rods. Near the windows hung great clusters of paper patterns. This was all legal, too.

On the eighth and ninth floors were two 30-gallon oil barrels and several hand cans. There was also some gasoline for removing spots. The floors were soaked with oil. Oily rags used in wiping the machines lay under the tables. Usually, a scrap-cloth dealer came every two weeks to collect the leftover material. But for some reason, the man who bought the Triangle's remnants hadn't been around since January. The scrap cloth and lint had just accumulated underneath the cutters' tables.

There were doors, stairs, and elevators on each side of the building. The girls usually left by the Washington Place side, and their handbags were examined to make sure that no textiles were smuggled out. The fact that the stairs were dark, narrow, and winding made no difference to them, for they never used the stairs. Fire buckets of water were on each floor.

There were no sprinklers. In New England, these were required before insurance could be obtained. But in New York, things were different. The Asch Building and its tenants were insured to a total of $1,647,000. The annual insurance fees came to $15,000. In a sprinkler-fitted building, the fees would have been only $1,100. Of this the brokers would have gotten a mere $60 commission. Therefore, the New York Fire Insurance Exchange, which was an absolute monopoly, rigged the rules so that sprinklers could *not* be installed! It was as simple as that. And quite legal.

On February 11, over a month before the fatal March 25,

the inspector of the New York Board of Fire Underwriters went through the Triangle plant. He found nothing wrong! The State factory inspectors, two weeks later, also found nothing wrong! The City Bureau of Buildings found nothing wrong! *After all, the building was fireproof, wasn't it?*

Almost everyone concerned seems to have been hypnotized by that one word—*fireproof*. Almost everyone seems to have forgotten that, although the building was fireproof, its contents and the workers were *not*.

One man who did not forget was New York City Fire Chief Edward Croker. Only the previous November, when fire in a Newark, N. J., factory building took 23 lives, the chief made this public statement:

"New York may have a fire as deadly as the one in Newark any time . . . There are buildings in New York where the danger is every bit as great . . . What we should have is an ordinance requiring fire escapes on every building used for manufacturing purposes. *Take, for instance, some of the large loft buildings below Twenty-third Street. The employees go up to their work in the elevators and many of them do not even know where the stairs are.* I have appeared before many committees trying to have the ordinance amended so that fire escapes would be required . . . The opposition has come in no little part from architects who fear the beauty of the buildings would be destroyed."

A meeting of the New York Manufacturers' Association had just lately been held in Wall Street to protest the proposed fire escape law. Who needs fire escapes on a "fireproof" building? The law didn't require it. But the architect of the Asch Building had put one in, anyway. Not on the outside; that would have been ugly. On the inside court, an air shaft cut off from the street by a high iron-spiked fence—that was where the single fire escape went. Chief Croker estimated that it would have taken *three hours* for the Triangle's 600 employees to get down the narrow iron stairs single file!

Shortly before 4:45, Max Blanck came back to his office from the sample room. There was a telephone call from the ground floor—a taxicab had arrived for his little girls and their nurse. "Tell him to wait," Blanck said. His work hours were longer than his employees'—he wanted to spend as much time with the children as possible. On the floor below, his partner, Isaac Harris, looked at his watch. "Ring, 'turn off power,' " he said.

Exactly what happened next will never be known. Perhaps a defective wire blew and shot a spark into some oily waste under the machines. Perhaps one of the men lit a cigarette and tossed away a still-lit wooden match. Max Rothen, working on the eighth floor, looked up suddenly and saw that the patterns overhead were ablaze. He jumped up and tore at the burning pieces, but some of them rose, flaming, into the air and floated—first up and then down—across the room onto the piles of cloth which were everywhere about.

Someone shouted, "*Fire!*" In an instant, the place was filled with smoke. The flimsy materials burned like tinder. Flames shot from bale to bale, from one fabric-piled table to another. Lace, linen, tissue paper, oily rags—there was no stopping the flames. Rothen emptied the row of water buckets, but it was like spitting into a furnace. Flames shot up all around him. He turned and was carried off in the first frenzied rush for the Greene Street stairs.

The women began to scream, and their screams ended in choking coughs as smoke billowed up all around. They jumped to their feet, and the tightly packed chairs and benches tripped them. They tried to flee, and their long skirts and sleeves caught in the machines. Flames came rolling across the oil-soaked floors and licked at them. Some women collapsed at their places and died there. Some ran for the stairs, others for the elevators. And many, many headed straight for the windows, flung them open, or shattered them with chairs, shoes, and bare hands.

The resulting rush of air fanned the fire into a holocaust. The flames rushed upward. The heat carried blazing bits of cloth up the stairways, like so many torches, to the ninth floor. Diana Lifschitz, at the telautograph, saw the ninth floor windows crack and splinter as the flames lapped in from below. Frantically, she sent the message, *The building is on fire, run for your lives!* Then she ran for hers. The stairs, too narrow for two people to go abreast, were dark and filled with smoke and fire, and soon became a death trap. A fleeing, screaming girl stumbled at the seventh floor. The girl behind fell over her. In a second the living, shrieking bodies were piled up like jammed logs. Those who trampled in panic over the fallen, fell and were trodden underfoot themselves.

The message girl on the tenth floor read the telautograph in amazement. "Say, is Diana stringing me?" she asked. Then she saw smoke coming up from below, and then the great bins of sample cards snapped into flame, and she screamed.

On all three floors, the hundreds of employees added their frenzied cries to the roaring of the fire. They darted in circles, seeking escape. Most of them had never used anything but the elevators, and it was toward the elevators that many now fled. Others, cut off by the blaze, rushed in terror for the windows. And some, barred from all other exits by the fire, rushed for the doors.

On at least one of the floors—the ninth—the Washington Place door could not be opened. And on all floors they opened inward. There was no chance to pull the door open on the eighth; in less than a minute, the press of bodies against it was too heavy. The girls beat upon it with their fists and screamed. Then a man seized the head of a sewing machine and broke open the top part of the door. Girls climbed through—were dragged through, torn and bleeding. Others who attempted to get through fell in the struggle and were trampled into the burning floor.

Now the terrible irony of fire in a fireproof building was made plain. The flames, unable to eat through walls and ceiling, turned in upon the long rooms crammed with flammables—and terrorized girls—and whirled around like maelstroms. Steel, cement, and terra cotta resisted; cloth, wood, and flesh and blood could not. Anna Gullo, on the ninth floor, broke a window with a pail to get air—but more flames poured in. "We started to run all around, *but the flames came in all around . . .*" one girl explained later.

Before long even the girls began to burn. Earlier some had jumped in mindless panic. After that, they jumped because they had no choice.

A man tried to restrain one of them. She paused on the window sill and turned her head. "This way, they'll be able to identify me," she said—and stepped into space. Some said their prayers first. Some covered their eyes first. Some waited till their hair and clothes burst into flames. Some went out arm in arm with friends. Some made way for others who begged to go first. Some fought to go first.

But, sooner or later, they all went.

Anna Dougherty ran toward the fire escape, but someone seized her by the coat. It was Solly Cohen, an office boy. "Come onto the roof!" he shouted. "That's the only way!" With two other girls he persuaded to follow him, they got up the stairs.

Louis Brown, the machinist, coming down the stairs, and a policeman named Meehan, who had run up from the street, succeeded in breaking up the jam of women trapped at the seventh floor. It was too late to help those further up. And below the eighth floor there were only a few persons in the building.

Small, stocky Joseph Zito, one of the passenger-elevator men, lived nearby on MacDougal Street. After the last of the cloak makers and hatters from the lower floors left at 3 o'clock, Zito and Gaspar Mortillaro, the other lift-man on the Washington Place side, had had nothing to do but wait till 4:45 when the Triangle let out. Their cars were on the main floor and they were idly shooting the breeze.

Bells on all three upper floors started ringing, there was the noise of banging on the glassed-in panels of the shaft doors, then glass smashed and came falling down, and then the two heard the screams of *"Fire!"* Neither said a word, but both started up at once at full speed.

On the Greene Street side, Frank Formanek, one of the two freight-elevator operators, also started up. The other operator lost his head and ran away.

Falling glass continued to smash on the roofs of the ascending cars. The girls were pressing so hard against the eighth floor door that Zito had to push them back through the broken panes before he could open the doors. They poured in madly. He sped down as fast as he could, shoved the trembling women out, sped up again. Harris, on the eighth floor, shouted, "Get the girls out first! Any man tries to get in ahead, hit him!" Only a very few tried, and Zito struck them back.

Mortillaro went to the ninth floor. Blanck shouted to him, "Run her till she drops!" The crowd was screaming and struggling madly to get in. He and Zito jammed 30 girls into a car intended for only 10.

Behind the seething mass of people, Zito saw "great flames and clouds of smoke." On his third trip to the eighth floor, he could see the girls at the window sills, fire all around them. On his fourth trip, he heard screaming from the ninth floor and there he found a scene of even greater terror. Formanek, meanwhile, could make only two trips. The passenger elevators were fatally small; the freight elevators were fatally slow.

Harris and Blanck, Blanck's children, and 20 or 30 of those working on the tenth floor got onto the roof by climbing up a step-ladder and smashing the skylight. But most never thought of going *up*—they had always gone *down*. And soon, very soon, that means of escape had become as red hot as the flue of a blast furnace.

As Zito approached the eighth floor on his fifth trip, the girls began jumping onto the car roof before he reached the landing. He saw that the doors there were now wide open, and feared the girls there would fall into the shaft if he went higher. Flames had begun to lick at the shaft. As he started down again, the screams grew more frenzied—"*Come back! Come back up!*" Desperate girls jumped onto the roof of the descending car a floor—then two floors—then three, five, eight floors below. Zito moaned as he heard the thud-thud-thud of bodies hitting the iron grating of the roof, and the clatter of silver coins from their pay envelopes as they rained down upon him.

Formanek's last trip was to the eighth floor. He had to grope with his hands to find the door in the dense smoke. "Going down!" he yelled. "Is anybody there?" No one answered. Choking and coughing, he went down alone.

Mortillaro reported that "women pulled my hair, dived on top of me, climbed on the roof. I must have carried forty on the last trip down. I had too much on the car." He wept. "They were grabbing my hands and jabbing me in the face, and then the car gave way. I don't know what I hit. The door wouldn't close and all the glass came down on top of me. They fell on me. They jumped on my roof. Their blood was on me." Flames ate at the cable, and his car ran no more.

Frank Steinberg, an N.Y.U. law student, saw Formanek's partner running through Washington Place, and recognized him as the freight-elevator man. "*Fire! Fire!*" the man shouted. Steinberg pulled the fire alarm box and then rushed into the building, where he ran the deserted car for four trips before the overheated cables failed.

Only a single cloud of smoke hung over the building. It was shot through with flames.

Zito, overcome by heat and smoke, staggered weeping into the street. From the crowd outside, a man named John Gregory darted forward. "You can't go in there," he was told. Gregory pushed past, shouting as he ran that he knew how to run an elevator.

By this time, the survivors crowded around the doors of the shaft had been driven insane from terror. "Their eyes stared from their heads in fear," Gregory recalled. "It was frightful. They were clinging to the wire netting with their hands and teeth. Their clothing was torn from their bodies. Some were

crushed to death. It was a mad fight for life . . . They were screaming and making flying leaps inside over the heads of others."

He ran the car till he was half-dead himself. He stopped only
when the mechanism of the car failed on its way down at the
third floor. He and the passengers ran down the stairs to the
street. This was the last car.

That Gregory's car stuck was not the fault of Thomas Horton,
the Negro porter who kept the machines which ran the elevators
going in the basement. The engineer fled at the first alarm. But
Horton toiled away in semidarkness, putting in switch cables till
they were disabled with water, and circuit breakers till they blew
out.

Into the flame-shot smoke of the now useless shafts the
women continued to jump. Some attempted to grasp and slide
down the cables. Several succeeded. One, reaching the bottom,
felt something move under her foot. "Please don't step on me," a
battered girl whispered. Then she died.

Natie Weiner slid down nine floors. So did Cecelia Walker.
Catherine Rubinowitz tried to persuade Kate Altman to join her
in the attempt, but Kate grew hysterical. "I want to be saved!" she
screamed, broke away, and jumped out of a window.

Sam Lavine started down from the ninth floor, and was slowly
braking his descent when a girl jumped and struck his back as
she fell. Lavine shot down to the bottom. His hands were ripped
to the bone but he lived. Hyman Meshel slid from the tenth floor
to the basement, where he clung to the cable drum, unable to
move, for hours.

Prof. Frank A. Sommers had a class of 25 on the tenth floor
of the N.Y.U. Law School, adjacent to the Asch Building. He was
explaining the New Jersey Civil Code when he heard what he
thought at first were the cries of skylarking students. Then he
saw smoke. He and his students rushed into the hall, where
two ladders were standing. They took these to the roof, 15 feet
higher than the roof of the Asch Building. With students guid-

ing them, over 50 women and 20 men escaped this way. Only one man, panic-stricken, rushed his way through the screaming women. As he reached the top of the ladder, students seized him and hurled him back.

On the Law School's ninth floor, 40 girls were listening to Prof. H. G. Parsons lecture on gardening. Parsons heard the same cries that Sommers did. He stepped to the window and looked out into the air shaft. Then, white, he turned to his class. "Young ladies," he said, "let us file out quietly. There seems—" he struggled with his voice— "to be a disturbance next door." The students obeyed. All left the building.

In the library facing the shaft, George Goldstein, Nathan Abraham, and Louis Newman were quietly studying when windows in the Triangle factory suddenly burst open. Terrified faces appeared. *"Fire!"* they screamed. *"Save us! Help!"* The students managed to find ladders and pushed them across the court. Girls clambered out and started across. Then some, looking down, panicked and refused to move. Some lost their grip and fell, shrieking. While Abraham and Newman threw themselves onto their end of the ladder to keep it from falling, Goldstein crawled out and managed to pull a hysterical girl to safety.

But soon flames swept out, and the ladders had to be abandoned.

The building's single, 18-inch wide fire escape led from another window on the court. It was this narrow ladder that Fire Chief Croker later said could not have enabled all the employees to escape in less than three hours. It was almost instantly jammed with employees so frantic to escape that at the eighth floor they bent the railings out of shape at the first rush. Some managed to reach the ground, or to break the windows into other floors. Others were trampled. Many plummeted to death on the sharp spikes of the courtyard fence.

On a lower floor, A. D. Feldman, a hatter, had stayed to close up. "It was appalling," he said. "The screams of the girls. I have never heard anything like it before, and hope I may never again." He flung open his shutters and pulled in those few who had gotten that far. Among them was Carmella Vetere, who had stumbled down from the ninth floor, shielding her face from the flames with her wide hat. As Feldman helped her, she burst into tears.

"My hat!" she wept. "My new hat . . ."

After her, a young man staggered in, covered with blood. "My friend?" he mumbled. "Where's my friend?" He didn't seem to notice a dead man on the grating.

Meanwhile Professor Parsons had taken the look into the court which he never forgot. "I saw a fire escape literally gorged with girls from the ninth to the first floor," he said. "Then it seemed to tear loose from its fastenings. The weight of all those bodies . . . Some of them fell. They tumbled like paper dolls, end over end, to the pavement. Some clung to the dangling ladder, screaming. And, as I watched, I saw a great tongue of flame reach out and sweep the fire escape from top to bottom. Then the girls who had been there dropped out of my sight like flies over the mouth of a furnace.

"Not one escaped . . ."

At the start of the blaze, James Cooper, the *World* reporter, stood waiting. It seemed to him that no one was in the building, and he said as much to another onlooker.

"What the hell, it's fireproof, ain't it?" the man observed.

Then "something that looked like a bale of dress goods" came hurtling out of an eighth-story window. "*Some*body's there," the man with Cooper said. "He's trying to save the best goods." A small crowd had collected. Almost at once a second "bundle of cloth" came flying down. The wind caught the fabric and seemed to open it. A single cry of horror arose from the crowd.

"*It's a girl!*" Cooper shouted. "*Look!*" he screamed, pointing. "*Look!*"

A third girl had broken open a window with her fist and leaped onto the window sill. "*Don't jump!*" the crowd screamed. "*Don't jump!*" But her long hair streamed in the wind and her hair was all on fire as were her clothes. She flung out her arms and leaned forward. For a split second she stayed so. Then, as the crowd moaned, she came down.

And after that three more jumped. And then, for a while, no more.

"Where are the fire engines?" someone shouted. The alarm box was pulled repeatedly.

Three or four girls could be seen now, leaning out the eighth-story window, waving their arms and shouting for help. Then one seemed to just slip out and fall. A great gust of flame poured out after her. A policeman from the Eighth Precinct House in Mercer Street ran up as she struck the street and rolled limply to rest next to the bodies of her friends.

"My God, where are the firemen?" the policeman yelled, and ran back to find a phone. He missed seeing two more girls leap, their arms around each other.

Office workers watching from the upper windows of the buildings across the street now saw hundreds of girls rushing to the windows on the Washington Place side of the ninth and tenth floors of the Asch Building. Until then there had been no indication from outside that the fire had reached the two top floors. Now smoke puffs appeared rapidly, and then a girl leaped right through the glass of a tenth-story window, and flames began to dance there.

More police arrived. "At least let's carry away the bodies," men in the crowd begged. But falling glass and pieces of cornices were raining down, and the police formed a line. "We would all go, if it would do any good," a sergeant said. "But the wall may come down. Stand back there. Stand—"

He paused. The clang of a fire bell sounded from Broadway and a cheer went up from the crowd. It died down almost at once as the apparatus was seen to be only a chemical wagon, useless at so large a fire. Then the hook-and-ladder company arrived. Girls on the sills and ledges were seen to turn their heads to tell those inside that rescue had arrived.

The ponderous ladder swung up—two floors—three—five—

And there it stopped.

The building was 10 floors high, but the fire ladder reached only to the fifth.

Even so, a girl leaped for it—and caught it! At once, the firemen raced up toward her, but she lost her grip and fell. A fireman on the ground darted over and beat out her burning hair with his hands. Then he got up. "It's no use touching her now," he said.

Now those who had managed to escape by the stairs came pouring out of the building. Some wept, some fainted. At that moment the first ambulance from Bellevue Hospital came up with a clatter of hooves; behind it, one from St. Vincent's; and first aid stations were set up at the corner.

"The climax of the terror in the street came just as the first water tower came dashing up," Cooper reported. "While the tower was scarcely one block distant three girls leaped from the tenth story . . . Hundreds of women were in the crowd and their nerves gave way at this latest horror. Three fell fainting at my feet."

Police whistles shrilled everywhere; the wailing of sirens, the screams of the trapped workers, and the shouts of the horrified spectators filled the smoky air.

"At the westward window of the ninth floor, a girl appeared, standing on the lower ledge," the *World* man noted. "Stretching her arms in an appeal for help, she seemed to study the crowd below. The window was outlined with little tongues of flame. One touched her dress and she began to burn. Again stretching out her arms, she plunged head foremost to the street."

Now the ponderous water tower began to swing into place. Hoses were rapidly strung across the street. Before they could be put to work, so many bodies had fallen onto them that they were rendered useless and a second line was rigged up. The water was turned on and the huge streams began to play, passing the ladders leaning uselessly against the fifth floor. The force of the water broke windows at the sixth floor. The watchers waited for it to reach the three top floors.

The gushing torrents reached the seventh story. And could reach no higher.

The Fire Department's equipment filled the street. But it could not save a single life.

From the ninth floor, Ida Singer jumped. Her skirt caught in a projecting sign at the sixth floor. She hung there, limp. Then she grasped the coping and pulled herself in through the window.

As the flames roared, the rain of bodies became more furious.

"The sound of the fearful impact, which came like a hail of death, caused men to hide their faces and women to sink to their knees," one horrified watcher recalled. "The firemen shouted and gesticulated to them not to jump. The clothes of the victims were blackened, contrasting with the pallor of their faces. There was no time to perform the offices of the dead . . . uncovered, they lay with their faces to the sky.

"Three young women conversed with each other on a ledge, as if advising the best course. One looked back into the room from which volumes of smoke were pouring and shook her head, while the faces of the others took on an agonizing look. They braced themselves to hold their positions. Then a sheet of flame shot out and enveloped them in fire. Their bodies toppled, hair and clothes aflame, but locked in each others' arms, they never separated as they dropped to the pavement."

Such was the force—equivalent to 14 tons—with which they struck the "deadlights" set into the pavement that the glass shattered in pieces and the bodies plunged, blazing, into the basement. Coroner Holghauser burst into tears.

At first, attempts had been made to catch the leaping victims in life nets. But even when they jumped one at a time, the bodies hurtled through the tough canvas as if it were cheesecloth and were crushed on the sidewalk.

"The sight of so many human beings dashed to pieces sickened the crowd, and the shrieks of the victims and of hysterical onlookers made the scene one of indescribable horror," an observer reported. "Hell can't be worse than this."

And still, long after it seemed no one could remain alive in the blazing inferno, girls continued to appear at the windows. It was vain to shout, "Don't jump!" With elevators and stairs cut off, fire escape torn loose, what else could they do?—except remain to be burned alive.

On the ledge at the ninth floor, a man and woman were seen to embrace. Then they jumped. *"They jumped, they crashed through broken glass, they dashed themselves to death on the sidewalk!"* So a New York *Times* reporter summed up the dreadful scene.

Some few of the women had torn off their clothes in real or fancied terror that they were afire, others had them torn off in the frenzied struggles to reach the windows. When these naked or near-naked forms fell to their death, spectators broke through police lines to dart over and cover the still white forms with coats. And some other women, modest even at the last, had pinned their skirts together so that their bodies should not be exposed as they fell.

Heaps of bodies lay scattered on sidewalks and streets. Torrents of water from hoses and fire towers fell upon the limp figures, and for a long while these waters ran red. But soon there was no blood left to stain them.

Word of the disaster spread rapidly through the poverty-stricken and crowded streets of the Lower East Side, where most of the Triangle employees lived. At once, their families hurried to the scene by horsecar and on foot, terrified at what they might find. The crowd, swelled to thousands, repeatedly charged the police lines and was repeatedly forced back. As the fire died down, many of the curiosity seekers departed. But all that cold March evening the families waited. And waited.

Finally, the firemen were able to couple together hoses and get close enough to douse whatever still smoldered. And then the work of removing the bodies began. At first, it was thought that no more than 25 bodies would be found inside. Then the bodies in the airshaft were found. Then the bodies piled in the elevator shafts . . . then those huddled around the door on the ninth floor, the bolt still shot in the burned doorframe . . . the bodies still crouched over their sewing machines . . .

Each corpse was wrapped in canvas and tied. Then it was swung out the shattered windows on a block-and-tackle. At each floor, a fireman was poised to keep the remains clear. Huge searchlights illuminated the night, and the distorted shadows of firemen and shrouded bodies were cast—vastly magnified— on the building opposite. At the foot of the building each body was tagged and placed in a coffin, then transferred to a waiting ambulance and taken to the department's pier at the foot of East 26th Street.

At 1 o'clock Sunday morning, the waiting ones were admitted in batches of 20. The lines reached all along 26th Street, down First Avenue, and far into 18th Street. Slowly, the small groups filed past the coffins and steeled themselves to look. Police reservists kept many from flinging themselves into the river as soon as they recognized their dead. Screams echoed from the shabby walls. Many fell insensible. Others nodded numbly. Identification in some cases could be made only by wisps of hair, fragments of clothes, a shoe, an earring.

Serafino Maltese identified his sisters Lucy and Sarah. Hysteria was a luxury he could not allow himself—he had still to find the body of his mother. Rose Salomon looked only at the hands of the victims, averting her gaze from the faces. At coffin number 34, she stopped. She thought the ring looked familiar. "Is there a watch?" she asked. There was. It was opened. Inside was her own picture. It was her fiancé, Joseph Wilson. She fell, shrieking, to the floor.

Harry Marks was looking for a ring on a girl's hand. He didn't find it. As he was about to leave, a policeman wordlessly pointed to coffin number 40. Attached to it was a tiny purse. The ring was inside. Marks fell on his knees beside the coffin, weeping in anguish.

And so it went. As soon as identification was made, the undertakers were allowed to remove the body. But as the hearses rolled past those still waiting to get in, many, fearful lest mistakes in identity had been made, rushed screaming at the black wagons and tried to peer into the coffins.

The total number of dead was finally listed at 147. Of this, seven bodies remained unidentified. The Waist Makers Union asked to be allowed to bury them, but the police—fearful, perhaps, of civil commotion—refused to allow this. The nameless victims were buried in one grave at Greenwood Cemetery, while Jewish, Protestant, and Roman Catholic services were held over them.

But the labor groups held the funeral procession with an empty hearse drawn by six white horses draped all in black. For hours, the 50,000 marchers passed through lower Manhattan in the cold rain. Each group bore two signs—one a banner reading *We Mourn Our Loss*—the other a simple triangle.

"The guilty parties will be punished!" The fire chief, the fire marshal, the fire commissioner, the buildings commissioner, the district attorney, the mayor, the governor—everyone spoke of "guilt" and "punishment." The Italian consul-general was severe. The labor unions were relentless. When so many are dead, so many stricken with grief, *somebody has to be guilty*. Suspicion first, then anger, then outrage, fell finally on the owners of the Triangle factory, Blanck and Harris.

A door on the ninth floor had been found locked. Blanck and Harris had forbidden the employees to leave by that door. Therefore, so ran the growing swell of accusation. Blanck and Harris must have locked that door! They were indicted on charges of first and second degree manslaughter in the death of a Margaret Schwartz and were brought to trial in mid-December.

Little in the appearance of the defense attorney, Max Steuer, suggested that he was reputed to be a "cross-examination genius," or that judges sitting on other cases sometimes adjourned to go and hear him; but so it was. The defense was that the door had been closed, not locked, and that the key was fastened to the doorknob by a string. How then, had it become locked? The defendants didn't know. It was suggested that someone, failing to open it in those first panic-stricken seconds, had assumed it *was locked*, and had turned the key in it, thus really locking it.

But there was no proof.

The prosecution kept its most damaging witness, a girl named Katie Amsterdam, for last. Her story was a dreadful one. She described how, when the fire broke out, she had run into the ladies' room and wet her hair at the sink. She ran out of there and joined the rush to the door, where she saw Margaret Schwartz on her knees. When the latter's hair and dress caught fire, the witness said, she—Katie—somehow managed to escape and run back into the main room.

"I jumped on a table," she said to the hushed courtroom. "I saw Bernstein, the manager's brother, jumping to the windows like a wildcat, then he ran back . . . then he went out the window . . . the Greene Street door was like a wall of flame . . . Finally, I made up my mind, and I ran through the fire with a cloth over my head, and I escaped by the stairs . . ."

The spectators shuddered. But Steuer's experienced ear had noted something in her account. When it came time to cross-examine, he began with quiet, inconsequential questions. Where did she live now? In Philadelphia? How long had she been in New York?

Finally: "Tell us again, please, Katie, where you were when the fire broke out."

Katie told him. Then, "I ran into the ladies' room and wet my hair at the sink. I ran out of there and tried to get out by the Washington Place door . . . Margaret Schwartz was on her knees . . . her hair and clothes started to burn . . . somehow I managed to escape. . . I jumped on a table . . . Bernstein, the manager's brother, was jumping to the windows, then he ran back . . . then he went out the window . . . the Greene Street door was like a wall of fire . . ."

When she was done, Steuer said, quietly, "Katie, you left out three words."

"I did?"

"Yes, you left out the part about Mr. Bernstein jumping 'like a wildcat.'"

"Oh, yes" said Katie.

Once again, Steuer asked questions, unconnected with the fire. And once again he asked her to tell the story again. "I ran into the ladies' room and wet my hair . . ." she repeated. "Margaret Schwartz was on her knees . . . Bernstein . . . jumping to the windows like a wildcat . . . I escaped by the stairs."

It was by then obvious that she had memorized her story, and this meant only one thing; she had been coached.

Judge Crain said to the jury: "I charge you that before you find these defendants guilty of manslaughter you must find, beyond a reasonable doubt, that this door was locked with a personal knowledge of the defendants."

The jury acquitted them on the third ballot.

Said one bitter headline: 147 DEAD, NOBODY GUILTY. And the Socialist *Call* declared that "The whole capitalist system is based on such unspeakable systematic murder, and those who defend the capitalists defend those murders."

The *Press* put it somewhat differently: "It was a blind passion for revenge and not a sound conviction that these men were exclusively responsible for the sacrifice of those lives, that inspired clamor for their conviction.

"The blood of those victims was on more than two heads; on more than twenty heads; perhaps on more than a million heads. Everybody connected with the actual neglect of the fire and building laws, whether in an official or unofficial capacity, shared in the blame."

So Blanck and Harris vanished into obscurity instead of into Sing Sing. But the laws were changed—fire laws, factory laws, workmen's compensation laws—a flood of new social legislation followed in the train of Triangle Fire.

The Asch Building (now the Brown Building) of N.Y.U. is still standing. It still has no outside fire escapes. After all, it's fireproof—isn't it?

THE FURNITURE FELLOW

CHICAGO POLICE CHIEF HUGHES looked at the business card on his desk, then looked up again at the young man on the other side. "All right," he said, "I'm listening."

Assistant State's Attorney William H. McSwiggin leaned forward eagerly. It was 1922; the Volstead Law, Prohibition's enabling act, was only a little more than two years old, and it was still possible for a young man in his position to be eager.

"This Joe Howard," he said, "was just a hoodlum. I think someone must've given him the idea, he was too dumb to think of it himself. He got on top of a truckful of hooch and draped a blanket in front of the windshield. Naturally the driver stopped, Joe jumped him, and drove off with the truck and sold the stuff.

"Since it was so easy, he tried it again. Then he began to boast about how he was an ace hijacker. He was shooting off his mouth that night in Heinie's saloon. Three witnesses saw a man come in, heard Joe say, 'Hello, Al,' heard the shots. Five of them. That's the end of Joe Howard. That's the end of my case, too, it looks like."

"With three witnesses? Who described him so perfectly we were able to pick him up the next day? How come?"

McSwiggin shrugged. "They all came down with galloping amnesia. 'You said he was heavily built, with a pudgy face.' 'I don't remember.' 'You said he had a long scar on the right cheek.' 'I don't remember.' Look, Chief—you've got men who know how to jog reluctant witnesses. How about helping me out here?"

Hughes pursed his lips, picked up the card and read it aloud.

Alphonse Capone

Second Hand Furniture Dealer

2220 South Wabash Avenue

Chicago, Illinois

"Now there you know he *can't* be on the level!" the younger man burst out. "He was the bouncer in the Four Deuces when Big Jim was still around, this Al was. Anybody complain the dice were loaded, or some broad picked his pocket the time his pants were off, Al knocks him down, kicks him in the crotch, throws him out. Now, all of a sudden, he moves to the corner store in the same building, and he's a furniture dealer! Why the Hell should Heinie and the other witnesses clam up for a furniture dealer— or a bouncer, for that matter?"

The Chief raised patient eyebrows. The young man subsided. "You're old Sergeant McSwiggin's son, aren't you? Yes . . . I know Anthony. A good man. Well, my boy, I'll see what I can do."

With thanks and a handshake, Assistant State's Attorney McSwiggin left the office. He never got his witnesses to talk and so he never got his indictment. In the end, however—an end then nine years away—and in the most indirect way conceivable, it was McSwiggin who was to be responsible for the downfall of "Alphonse Capone, Second Hand Furniture Dealer." And five hundred men were to follow Joe Howard to a bloody death, without a single conviction for murder, in Chicago during that not-quite-decade. Not since the legendary Old Man of the Mountain pulled his last caper and turned up his damask-slippered toes had there been anything even remotely like it. With Hassan Sabbath-Shab it was hashish. With Al it was booze. His ship came in on a flood tide of bootleg liquor—and was wrecked just as that tide showed signs of ebbing.

But as for Police Chief Hughes and his promise to "see what he could do" about convicting Capone—it didn't take him long to see. The scarfaced killer outlasted four Chicago chiefs of police, and they all knew just what they could do to convict Capone:

Nothing. Not a damned thing.

The FBI file on Al Capone, America's most famous criminal, is complete in all respects save one. The line after the word *Birthplace* is blank. No one can say with certainty just where the future Shah of Chicago was born that 17th of January, 1899—except the Capone family, a notedly reticent clan. Alphonse himself allotted the honor to Brooklyn, but there seems good reason to think it may have been Naples. In 1899 only the Russian and Turkish empires required passports, so there is no proof either way.

Centuries of foreign oppression and poverty produced in Southern Italy and Sicily an anti-government emotion which sometimes became criminal. But Gabriele Capone and his wife Theresa were, like the overwhelming majority of their *paisani* in America, hard-working, law-abiding. The streets of the "alabaster cities" of the New World produced their own criminals. Gabriele fathered five sons and a daughter and died. Al was in the fourth grade. He could read—and once, years later, when he was in a Pennsylvania state prison, he read through a whole book to prove it—write, and count change. He left school right then.

"What did you like to do when you were a kid, Al?" a reporter once asked. The soft brown eyes lit up reminiscently. "I liked to dance," he said. "Boy, did I like to dance! Every Saturday night at the old Broadway Casino in Brooklyn—the Bunny Hug, the Turkey Trot—and high-class stuff, too. You know: the waltz, like."

On weekdays, when not engaged in whistling at the girls who passed by the corner of Broadway and Flushing Avenue, he put his time to such good use that before he was twenty he had been "questioned" in two murder investigations. The neighbors, later on, could never figure out how he came to be Chicago's Big Shot. A nice boy, yes. Agreeable, soft-spoken, but outstanding in nothing but dancing. One of them summed it up in turn-of-the-century slang. "Al," he said, "was just never fly."

And meanwhile, all unsuspecting, Chicago—"Hog butcher to the nation"—was waiting. It didn't have long.

The year was 1919. That monumental piece of stupidity, the 18th Amendment, was all set to go into effect. After which, presumably, America's millions would stop drinking. But in Chicago there was a man didn't who think so. His name was Johnny Torrio. He had connections in New York, he heard of Al, he sent for Al.

Officially, the twenty-year old Capone was to be bouncer at the Four Deuces—2222 South Wabash Avenue—part saloon, part gambling-den, part whorehouse. But if Johnny didn't exactly say, "Stick with me, kid, and you'll be wearing diamonds," he implied it. The Four Deuces was Torrio's headquarters. He'd been nine years older than Al was now when, in 1910, Big Jim Colosimo, boss of the teeming First Ward, brought him in as bodyguard. Johnny was a man with vision—of a special sort. One man with vision might consider the automobile and open a Ford agency. Johnny Torrio considered the automobile and opened a roadhouse. He stocked it with liquor, gambling equipment, dames and pay-off money.

By 1919 his roadhouses were all over "Chicagoland," which included northern Indiana, and gosh how the money rolled in. Somehow, Johnny Torrio believed that Prohibition, far from hurting business, was going to help it as never before. And he wanted somebody he could trust to help him help it. In short, Al Capone.

The New York kid who came to the Four Deuces (where twelve unsolved murders took place) was on the heavy side, but it was muscle, not fat. He stood five-eight and weighed a hundred-ninety pounds. He smiled and talked real friendly. He had thick, fleshy lips, a flat nose, not much neck, a bullet head, beetling brows, a thick jaw, and a long scar on the right cheek.

An odd thing is that, while he never willingly allowed the scarred side of his face to be photographed, and hated like poison to be called "Scarface," he had never borne any ill will to the man who had done it to him. "He was from the Old Country," Al shrugged it off, "and didn't know no better."

Big Jim Colosimo, Torrio's *padrone*, liked good food, good wine, good diamonds, and bad women. Preferably a blonde one, preferably tall and plump. He was mad about opera. So, for that matter, was Al himself. They got along famously. And when, in March of 1920, Big Jim, the street-cleaner who made good, took a bullet in his head, Al felt terrible. However, all was for the best in this best of all possible worlds.

"The old man was too soft-hearted and old-fashioned for these days," he pointed out to Torrio. 'To operate in Prohibition, it requires a different approach."

"The slayer," to use a favorite newspaperism—one to be used five hundred times in Chicago in the next ten years—"was never apprehended." And the firm of Colosimo and Torrio became the firm of Torrio and Capone. Before long the smiling kid's acquaintances in Chicago stopped referring to him as "Boxcar," a reference to his big and high-buttoned yellow shoes which made him unhappy. They began to call him "The Fellow." Eventually it was to be "The Big Fellow."

How did he make it to the top? For one thing, by conjecturing that there *was* a top. The bootleg liquor business in the earlier twenties was in much the same shape as the kerosene business was in 1870 when a pious Baptist bookkeeper went into it. There were a lot of firms in the business. In fact, there were too many. It was inefficient. John D. Rockefeller's ideas weren't too far away from those of Alphonse Capone. The Fellow, in his climb toward being The Big Fellow, didn't call his outfit Standard Moonshine —but the idea was the same: eliminate competition. And there was no Sherman Anti-trust Act, no meddling Supreme Court, to interfere with Al. Old John D. lived longer, but it is doubtful that he had as much fun.

Al didn't try to undersell, he didn't offer rebates, he didn't organize holding companies. The Capone drive toward monopoly was simpler. His gorillas were given a list of speakeasies, drug stores, groceries, soda fountains—every booze outlet in a given area. One by one they visited the outlets.

"Who ya getcher stuff from?" was the first question—a formality, really, as it didn't matter who, anyway, seeing it wasn't from Al—yet. And the second question was, "How about gettin' it from Us?" Those who declined this tempting offer were treated to a prompt course of the three Ms—menace, molestation, and massacre. Gradually the number of those declining died down. "Died," in fact, is exactly the right verb. It is just a bit surprising that it took seven years to complete Capone's monopoly of the Chicago booze trade. Some of his competitors were real hard-noses.

Al began to wear a fresh rose in his buttonhole. He bought an 11 1/2-carat diamond ring valued at $50,000. He gave away the yellow button shoes and took to having his footgear custom-made. And in the barber shop favored with his trade he had a special chair installed. It didn't pivot, it always faced the door. Who knew what uncouth characters might come barging in, bound on rude errands? But on those days that Al didn't report for a shave, the barber knew there had been a gangland slaying (no one was ever merely "killed" in gangland, he was "slain"). From the kill to the funeral Al never shaved. Why? Al never said. Great men have these foibles.

It mustn't be thought that because he was ruthless in business Capone had no warm feeling for human relationships. On the contrary. For example, for ten years he and his wife and son lived in the same house in Chicago with his mother, his sister, and his brother. It was only people who gave him a hard time that Al felt obliged to get tough with. He would much *rather* spend his time listening to opera, particularly *Aida*—he loved Radames' tenor arias—*Rigoletto*, and *Il Trovatore*.

About this time there was located, in "a sedate-looking residence" at 2146 South Michigan Avenue, the premises of a gentleman identified by the brass plate as a Doctor Brown. The waiting room even had copies of *Life*, *Judge*, *The Literary Digest*, and *National Geographic*. If anyone was naïve enough to apply to Dr. Brown for relief of a catarrh or a quinsy of the bowels, he was politely informed that "the Doctor" was a pharmacolo-

gist. His attention first directed to the shelves of sample bottles of medicaments, and then to the door. "Doctor Brown" was
the semi-professional name of a gentleman once in the second-
hand furniture business, and if he didn't sell celery tonic, he sold
drinks much more popular in Chi.

Besides samples of his liquid merchandise (purchasers were
given samples to have tested, if they so desired), the Michigan
Avenue setup housed the headquarters of the commercial aspect of Capone's syndicate. Few offices of American business
were better organized. A clerical corps of twenty-five was kept
busy over the loose-leaf ledgers, card indexes, memorandum accounts and day books, and all the paraphernalia required by a
Great Corporation. It was a far cry from the recalcitrant saloon-
keeper puking his life's blood onto his sawdust floor to the neat
figures of double-entry bookkeeping.

"I got everything here," Al used to say, affectionately patting a
row of filing cabinets. "Everything on everybody." And the end of
his expensive cigar would glow at the thought.

More specifically, the files contained six kinds of data. First, a
list of all Capone customers, from big-name Chicagoans through
big hotels to the corner drug stores. Second, the names of all
cops and "prohibs" (Prohibition agents) on his payroll. Third, all
the channels whereby liquor was transmitted from rumrunning
ships via New York, New Orleans, and Miami. Fourth, details of
the management of his four big breweries. Fifth, brothels. Sixth,
saloons. There was a story that a seventh file existed, labeled
"Vengeance and Punishment," but this is probably romance. Al
could have kept this last account in his head. He had the head for
it.

But behind the modern office, with its typewriters and adding
machines, was a room furnished with a single table and on the
table was a pair of candlesticks and a book. No one knows what
became of the candlesticks, but the book is in the vaults of the
University of Chicago Library. Composed of a hundred-forty-five
parchment pages, it is known as *The Argos Lectionary*—Biblical
chapters written in ancient Greek—and is over a thousand years

old. Al wasn't much of a churchgoer, but when he had his boys swear allegiance to him, he liked to feel that it was on "the real thing." The blasphemy of the ceremony seems never to have occurred to him.

It was on Election Day, 1924, that Capone took over Cicero even more firmly than he ever took over Chicago. It hadn't been his idea, originally. "Ed Konvalinka thought it up," he conceded. "Smart boy, Ed." Konvalinka, a Cicero soda-jerk turned politician, presented his slate of candidates to the voters. Present, and helping the voters of the Chicago suburb to make up their minds to vote right, was a small army of Capone's hoods. Armed. Konvalinka's men won by a landslide and Cicero tumbled into Capone's lap just as easy. He owned it, owned its mayor and council, its police force, and—not least of all—owned its saloon keepers. Almost overnight the once quiet town blossomed out with dog tracks and gambling houses. They were Al's, too . . . The election, it is interesting to note, was held on April Fool's day.

Next to become a Capone fief was Stickney, adjoining Cicero to the south. Stickney became wide-open for whorehouses. And in every one of the gambling dens, brothels, and dram shops was an agent of Al Capone and, of course, though he was getting on in years (he was forty-four), Johnny Torrio. From a quarter to a half of the gross went to Al and Johnny. By July, 1924, Al and Johnny were pocketing $100,000 a week each. It gave Al lots of room to move around at the crap games.

"He loved them dice," recalled an old Chicago hand not long ago. "He was one red-hot crapshooter—stay up all night, rip his shirt open, drop money all over the floor! He never cared if he won or not. It was the excitement he loved..."

And then there was Dion O'Bannion.

When Al was still just The Fellow, Dion was The Big Fellow. The son of a poor plasterer, he reigned over the Forty-Second and Forty-Third Wards of Chicago, ranging from the lake-front Gold Coast to the slums near the Chicago River. He had been indicted four times for burglary and robbery, but had never been tried.

The police had long been convinced that he was a murderer, but nothing had been done to convince him that crime did not pay, either. His official profession was that of florist. There is no evidence that Al loved second-hand furniture, but Dion loved flowers, and had a deft hand with the blooms. His shop was at 738 North State Street, opposite Holy Name Cathedral, where O'Bannion had once been an altar boy.

He had a build like an athlete's—broad shoulders, narrow waist, slender. His hands were small and delicate. His face was round and always smiling. Owing to an old accident, he limped and rolled when he walked. His eyes were blue. But just as the limp destroyed the effect of Dion O'Bannion's build, so the happy effect of face and smile was destroyed by his habit of cocking his head to one side. The general effect was one of slyness. He had been persuaded by Johnny Torrio to join forces with Johnny and Al (who hadn't been overjoyed), and owned a big slice of the Cicero saloon trade, in addition to his Chicago booze territory. O'Bannion himself never drank.

"I hate the filthy stuff!" he said.

Dion had his own distinctive habits, too. For one thing, he was ambidextrous, and carried three guns in specially-built pockets. His quick temper was all-embracing. When Nails Morton, his chief machine-gunner, was fatally kicked by a horse, O' Bannion had the horse shot.

In November of the eventful year of 1924 Michaele Merlo, the founder and president of the Chicago branch of the *Unione Sicilione* (widely known as the Mafia), died. He was the last holder of that office to expire of natural causes. Hs was given a funeral worthy of a bishop, including a lifesize wax effigy which was dressed in his clothes and rode in his car; cost: $5,000. Two men, one of whom was James Genna, of the Genna brothers who appear later on in Capone's history, came in to give O' Bannion an order for flowers for $750.

"Stay here," said Genna, as he left. "There's more orders coming." Dion nodded, went on snipping roses. In less than half an hour a blue Jewett sedan drove up. One man stayed at the wheel, three went inside.

"Hello, boys," Dion sang out, cheerfully. "You from Mike Merlo's?" He held out his right hand.

"Yes," said the center man of the three, taking the proffered right. The man to his left seized O' Bannion's left hand. The man to his right fired six bullets into him, as follows: two in the right breast, one in the larynx, one in the throat proper, one in the right cheek, one in the left cheek. Not very surprisingly, this proved more or less instantly fatal. The three men walked out to the blue sedan and drove off.

O'Bannion had his three guns on him at the time. The trouble was that he didn't have three hands.

Dion O'Bannion's funeral made history. His lieutenants, Bugs Moran and Earl Weiss, decided that the best would have to be bettered. A $10,000 casket was shipped from the East by special express freight car. It was, observed a lady reporter, "equipped with solid silver and bronze double walls, inner-sealed and airtight, with heavy plate glass above and a couch of white satin below, with a tufted cushion for his left hand to rest on." Here she paused for breath, and continued, "At the corners were solid silver posts, carved in wonderful designs."

Johnny Torrio was horrified—or, at least, terrified. "Al, Al," he groaned, "it should of never been done! I don't like it."

Al shrugged. "He was too undependable," he said. "Look what he done to that poor horse. And besides, he owned too big a slice of Cicero . . . We'll send him some nice flowers. He'd like that."

In charge of the murder investigation was Detective Captain William Shoemaker, a character right out of the movies, known to one and all as "Old Shoes." But comical or not, Old Shoes had sharp eyes. "When O' Bannion talked to strangers," he rumbled, "he stood with his feet apart, his right hand at his hip, his left in his coat pocket, ready for instant action with the automatic in the special pocket. If Dion O'Bannion walked up to three men with his hand out, it could mean only one thing. He knew them. And he didn't suspect them."

The Cook County Coroner marked the O'Bannion file, "Slayers

not apprehended. John Scalise, Albert Anselmi, and Frank Yale suspected, but never brought to trial." *Slayers not apprehended.* Of course not. Not in Chicago during the Capone Decade. And the world watched, and the world wondered.

One reason why the three were not apprehended and brought to trial was that Al couldn't spare them. Frankie Yale was an important man at the New York end of Al's booze business. Scalise and Anselmi were Al's two most faithful torpedoes, under whose skilled hands the "handshake murder" was brought to a pitch of perfection. It was that old efficiency, all over again.

Meanwhile, back at the funeral . . .

The undertaker was also a gentleman of another occupation. He was Assistant State's Attorney John A. Sbarbaro. He buried most of the big gangsters. He and another Assistant S. A., William McSwiggin, represented the State's Attorney's office in most of the investigations of gang fatalities. Sbarbaro, plainly, couldn't lose. McSwiggin, of course, had been watching Capone's career from the start.

"Silver angels stood at the head and feet of the coffin," the sob sister continued, "with their heads bowed in the light of ten candles that burned in solid gold candlesticks they held in their hands. Beneath the casket, on the marble slab which supports its glory, was the inscription, *'Suffer little children to come unto me.'*"

Johnny Torrio eased his collar with his finger, leaned over and whispered to Al, "The smell of all these flowers—it's choking me!"

Al, unshaven according to his custom for funerals, but resplendent in a new purple suit, muttered, "They cost $50,000! How much a sniff?"

Facing Johnny and Al were O'Bannion's three lieutenants, grim-faced: Bugs Moran, Earl Weiss (rosary in hand), and Vinny Drucci. A ten-piece orchestra played in Sbarbaro's funeral chapel. Ten thousand Chicagoans filed past the bier and jammed the streets, patroled by mounted police. Old Shoes and his men singled out and spoke to every gang leader and follower: "No shooting, boys. Only one funeral at a time."

It took 26 trucks to carry all the flowers, including an eight-foot-high heart of American Beauty roses, and a seven-by-ten blanket of roses, lilies, and orchids. There was also a huge arch of blossoms from which swung two white doves and a basket of red roses, *"From Al."*

Then it was over. Al shaved. Johnny Torrio ran like hell. To Hot Springs, New Orleans, the Bahamas, Cuba—he finally surrendered himself on an old liquor charge in a Wisconsin county and accepted a nine-month sentence. At his own expense he had the cell windows fitted with steel screens and hired three extra deputies for guards. Al stayed home to mind the store.

He minded it from the seclusion (if that is the word) of the swank Hotel Metropole on South Michigan Avenue, the Fifth Avenue of Chicago. Here Capone and Company had hired *fifty-four* rooms on the top three floors, well away from annoying street noises—and Bugs, Earl, and Vinny. They ran their own elevators, bars, and service kitchens. Gambling went on around the clock; call girls, important public figures, police, politicians, divekeepers and customers came and went in a steady stream. The wine cellar held $150,000 worth of liquor—"the pure quill," no hoked-up rotgut.

The man who once felt obliged to cloak his hooch dealings behind a second-hand furniture store front occupied suite No. 409-10, with a view of the Boulevard. At his right hand was his one-man brain trust, Jake "Greasy Thumb" Guzik, who kept in touch with every unit of the far-flung syndicate. Coded reports told him what was happening in Canada, Florida, New York, and points in between. It was estimated that the syndicate was grossing $30,000,000 a year.

By this time certain techniques of the business had become standard. For example, there was the poisoned bullet, rubbed with garlic, to promote infection in case the wound was not fatal. There was the dumdum bullet, a cross notched deeply in the soft lead nose. This made a huge and terrible wound. There was the blooey-gun—shotgun pellets were melted down to form a slug which was put back in the shell. The sawed-off shotgun which sprayed a wide target with death. The pineapple, or hand grenade. The belly-gun, a snub-nosed revolver pressed to the victim's stomach. This was useful for quick work in noisy crowds.

But perhaps the most characteristic weapon of the Capone era was the Thompson submachine gun, affectionately known as the Tommy gun. It fitted snug to the shoulder, there was a long piece for the non-shooting hand to hold and brace it, and the circular cartridge drum held fifty or a hundred bullets. The Tommy gun was also called the typewriter by virtue of its staccato rattle, and the drum had the nickname of ukulele. The submachine gun fitted neatly into a violin case. Some macabre musical pieces were played in those days.

(Al's chief master-at-arms was Machine Gun Jack McGurn, a clean-living killer who did his pushups regularly. There even was a legend that Capone himself had been "a doughboy with the A.E.F., operating a machine gun for Uncle Sam against the Hun hordes of Kaiser Bill in France." Not a sliver of proof was ever brought to back up this story—doubtless to the relief of the V.F.W.)

But it was Earl Weiss who invented the famous gangland technique of taking the victim "for a ride." Alive, and with guns pressed to his sides, he was driven to some rural retreat where the execution was carried out. If, for any reason, immediate discovery of the body was indicated, it was rolled into a barrel which was filled with cement.

The "sinful, ginful Twenties" were a jolly decade all right, filled with ingenious games. Prohibition had made the American people contemptuous of the law, and on that contempt men like Capone rode to power. A prominent Chicago lawyer was once present when Al delivered a tongue-lashing to a high-ranking judge.

"Why the hell wasn't Lewie sprung?" he yelled. "What'm I paying you for?"

"I'm sorry, Al," His Honor said. "The clerk was late with the writ of habeas corpus. It won't happen again."

"It better not," grumbled Capone.

Small wonder, then, that the cop on the beat looked the other way.

And then the O'Bannions struck back, like Japanese *ronin* avenging the death of their Samurai lord.

Crossing "No Man's Land"—Madison Street, which divided their territory from Capone's—in a long, black touring car with drawn curtains, Weiss, Moran, and Drucci came upon Capone's sedan. At a range of three feet they roweled it with Tommy guns from end to end, ruining the motor forever. The chauffeur was badly wounded. Capone? He had just stepped into a restaurant to use the men's room . . .

A week later the fearsome threesome caught up with Johnny Torrio, putting a .45 bullet in his left arm and giving him a load of buckshot that smashed his jaw and punctured his stomach and lungs. Displaying more courage than the whole Chicago police force, a seventeen-year-old boy three times identified Bugs Moran as the chief trigger. Nevertheless, Moran was released on only $500 bail. Who was the Assistant State's Attorney who asked for such low bail? None other than Sbarbaro, the busy undertaker.

Torrio, taking nourishment through a nose-tube, "true to the traditions of the underworld," named no one. But it is safe to say that he thought a lot.

So did Al. He had made to order a bulletproof sedan weighing seven tons and costing $20,000. Not even machine-gun bullets or shrapnel could penetrate it, let alone buckshot. It had double panes of bulletproof glass and a combination lock to keep anyone from depositing a bomb within. Furthermore, it traveled in convoy—a scout flivver in front and a touring car behind, each carrying a posse of sharpshooters. When Capone turned out for a first-night in the Loop, these hoods wore tuxes.

"Al," said Chicago *Tribune* reporter Jake Lingle, "you've got eighteen bodyguards when you go to the show, and the President of the United States doesn't rate that many."

The Big Fellow cackled. Then he scowled. "The President of

the United States don't have my worries," he said. This was undoubtedly true. Affairs of state weighed so lightly on Calvin Coolidge in those happy days that he managed to take a two-hour nap every afternoon on his office sofa.

"Does the President hafta wear a bulletproof vest?" Mr. Big demanded. "Does he hafta keep twenty lawyers eating their heads off on great big retainers? Does he hafta keep fifteen million bucks lying idle for emergencies—for grease-money?"

"Probably not," conceded Lingle. He was reputed to be taking in about $60,000 a year himself for acting as a link between the underworld and the lawfully constituted authorities. He was known, though not openly, as "The Mayor of the Loop"—the heart of Chicago's downtown area—and "the guy who fixed the price of beer in Chi."

Lingle knew plenty. And one of the things he knew was the reason why Capone didn't strike back at the Moran mob that two-year period of 1924-5. Al was having trouble with the Genna brothers, one of whom, it will be remembered, had fingered Dion O'Bannion for him. There were six of them, originally in Marsala, Sicily. Pete kept a saloon, Jim ran a blind pig, Sam specialized in blackmail and extortion, Mike was a strong-arm man, Antonio was a ward heeler, and Angelo was the brains.

Ninety per cent of the booze drunk in Chicago then was synthetic; that is, it was a mixture of raw alcohol and water, with coloring and flavoring added. At 1022 Taylor Street the brothers had an alky warehouse where they sold the stuff to wholesalers. "It was," complained a Chicago paper afterward, "as open as a department store." To prevent hijacking as well as raids by the law, the Gennas' trucks moved around under police convoys. They were so big that they could refuse to pay off any copper whose badge number wasn't on their list.

They were so big that they thought they could buck Capone.

In May of 1925 someone blew off Angelo's head with a blooey-gun. In June Al's top torpedoes, Anselmi and Scalise, took Mike for a ride. In July Antonio got the handshake murder. That tore it. Peter, Jim, and Sam took off for Sicily without stopping to change their sox.

The Gennas had been running the Chicago *Unione Sicilione*. Al now installed a pal of his named Lombardo as prexy of the Chi branch, and the *Unione* stayed quiet for a while. Al, in his Prairie Avenue home, was able to relax with his family, which now included a son, Al Junior. Al (Senior) puttered around in carpet slippers with a pink apron tied around his thickening middle while he cooked spaghetti for his folks and friends. "It's the oregano gives it the taste—but just a little," he said.

Another year of comparative peace went by. Al indulged in gestures like buying up newsboys' stocks with twenty-dollar bills. He could, shall we say, afford it. The Big Fellow never traveled with less than $50,000 cash on his pudgy person, and scattered largess to waiters, ushers, manicure girls, panhandlers, and assorted members of the multitude. There was always plenty more where that came from.

"Chicago's chief defect," proclaimed the Illinois Crime Survey, "has been in its very energy." Well, that was okay with Al. The more energy Chicago had, the more it boozed, whored, and gambled, the more it enriched Capone. He was all for the rude vigor of the nation's second largest city.

"Let the people live it up," he said, expansively. "What the hell, it's good for'm!" And for such of the people who didn't think that what was good for Capone was good for Chicago, why, there was always the blooey-gun, the belly-gun, the Tommy gun, the pineapple, the last ride.

Waiting for Al to act made the Moran mob nervous. By the summer of '26 they decided to take the advice of General Nathan Bedford Forrest, and "git there fustest with the mostest." Carefully, and with deliberate speed, they began to lay their plans.

Capone's Cicero headquarters were in the Hawthorne Hotel in the middle of the 4800 block on West 22nd Street, just past Chicago's western city line. It was the Big Fellow's custom to take a cup of coffee in the hotel's restaurant of an afternoon during the dog-track season. He was so engaged, in company with bodyguard Johnny Rio, when eight touring cars drove down West 22nd at fifty miles an hour.

The lead car drove a block ahead, sounding a police-car type gong and shooting off blanks. Those in the restaurant, not knowing they were blanks, hit the floor—Al and Rio among them. As the lead car drove off Capone started to his feet, only to be tackled by Rio. "It's a phony!" he shouted. "Stay down!"

Thirty seconds later the other seven cars came abreast of the block, ten feet apart, raking the hotel with bullets. The sixth car stopped in front of the hotel and played a Tommy gun on it. It used up two drums of the .45 shells which will cut down a twenty-four-inch wide tree at thirty feet and penetrate four-inch steel armor plate. Then the seventh car gave three honks of its horn and the attackers were off. There was no pursuit.

A thousand shots had been fired. Every window in the hotel had been shattered. The walls were pocked with bullets from waist to neck high. But no one, incredibly, had been killed! Worst injured was a Mrs. Freeman, an innocent car sitter, whose eye was damaged by flying glass. Capone voluntarily paid out $10,000 for medical bills for the unlucky lady.

Newspapers spoke, in terms approaching admiration, of "the soldierly precision" with which the raid had been carried out. But precision or not, it had failed.

O'Bannion's three *ronin* kept separate headquarters. Earl Weiss had his upstairs from the famous flower shop, which Dion's partner in the posy trade still maintained. Shortly after the Cicero raid a room was taken at 740 North State Street, two doors up. On October 5th a vigil was set, and it lasted till the afternoon of October 11th at three o'clock, when Weiss received ten steel-jacketed bullets. The killers casually walked away, leaving behind their arsenal of Tommy guns, sawed-offs, and revolvers.

Al refrained from shaving. Weiss's undertaker? Who else but that busy investigator of gangland slayings, Assistant State's Attorney Sbarbaro. "Geeze, I'm really sorry," said Al. "I heard I was, like, suspected, so I called up the detectives and asked did they wanna see me. They din't."

However, Detective Captain William "Old Shoes" Shoemaker had this to say: "Capone imported the killers of Weiss and rushed them out of town afterwards." And Bugs Moran (his real name was George) and Vinny Drucci said nothing. Nothing for publication, that is. They drew back a bit. Capone pushed forward a bit . . .

One night an odd trio got together in Cicero. There was Tom Duffy, beer-runner and Republican precinct captain; Jimmy Doherty, a hood recently tried for murder and acquitted—prosecutor? Assistant S.A. McSwiggin—and a third man, to wit, Assistant S.A. McSwiggin. Why they were together was never explained. As they got out of the car and started toward Harry Madigan's saloon there was the rattle of a typewriter. Not Remington—Thompson. All three slumped to the sidewalk dead.

There was a real clamor this time. A special prosecutor was appointed to investigate: ex-Judge Charles A. McDonald, who, with two assistants, impaneled no less than five special grand juries and collected $34,135 in pay. Result: "On the whole there is no special cause for alarm at the present moment. The situation is well enough in hand." This was 1926, when there were sixty-one *known* Chicago gang slayings—three indictments—and no convictions.

"The situation well in hand?" In Capone's hand, maybe.

Old Shoes traced three Tommy guns, found a brave witness, accused Al in a statement that made the front pages of the world. "Capone himself led the killers of McSwiggin," he charged. "There were five autos carrying nearly thirty gangsters. *Capone handled the machine gun himself*, being compelled to set an example of fearlessness to his less eager companions." And, perhaps, to take personal and long-delayed vengeance on the man who had first pressed a case against him?

Just to show that they were on the ball, the authorities raided The Ship, a top, Capone-controlled, Cicero gambling hall. They even impounded some of the books, which were turned over to the Internal Revenue people, who tossed them into a closet. Capone himself, stubble emphasizing the pink-red scar on his pallid cheek, hid out till his lawyers judged it safe. When the charge was dismissed, old Sergeant Anthony McSwiggin said, bitterly, "They pinned a medal on him and turned him loose."

And "Who killed McSwiggin?" became a Chicago byword.

On October 20th a "peace conference" was held at the Hotel Sherman, next to Chicago's City Hall and the police chief's office. Present and accounted for: Al Capone, Bugs Moran, *Unione Sicilione* president Lombardo, Vinny Drucci, and assorted scum. The following terms were agreed to by the signatory powers:

(1) General amnesty. (2) No more murders or beatings. (3) Past injuries forgotten. (4) Leaders to be responsible for men. (5) Moran and Drucci to stay in O'Bannion's old wards. (6) Everything south of Madison Street to Capone.

There was peace until December 30th. A punk named Clements then machine-gunned the beer barrels of a troublesome grog-seller, thus letting the merchandise run all over the floor. Clements, who was promptly shot, was one of Al's boys. *Boom!* The shooting started again!

The new year, 1927, saw the Chicago booze monopoly, for which Johnny Torrio's early vision had prepared Al, to be an accomplished fact. Torrio, his old wounds still troubling him, began to retire from active participation in the rackets. Government investigators estimated the syndicate revenues at $105,000,000 a year. The breakdown was like so: Beer, liquor, and "alky-cooking"—$60,000,000. Gambling, including dog-tracks—$25,000,000. Vice, dance halls, roadhouses, resorts—$10,000,000. Assorted rackets—$10,000,000.

Out of this Capone had to pay off the high and the low and meet his own payroll. "Why, the guy is lucky if he nets thirty million a year for his own pocket!" one cynic declared. Al himself decided to start the year with a trip to Hot Springs, Arkansas. Outside the spa-town a speeding car came tearing by and tossed a few slugs into Capone's machine, which was not the armored model. Al opened the far door and dropped like a bag of laundry into the ditch along the road.

It was his closest brush with death. "Leave this be a lesson to me," he said. "Al: stay outa the sticks!" When he paid a visit to Los Angeles and was invited by the police to leave town, he was surer than ever that his place was in Chicago. With Mayor William "Big Bill" Thompson sitting in City Hall, Capone felt he had nothing to worry about.

Big Bill didn't bother about "reform" or "chasing out the criminal element." His target, proclaimed with whoops and hollers, was the English Menace. "The English are trying to take over America!" he bellowed. "The library of the University of Chicago is filled with rotten, un-American, English propaganda, which they won't get away with it and I'll see it burned if it's the last thing I do! And as for King George—" he roared, red-faced and flailing the air with angry fists— "if he pokes his face inta Chicago, I'll punch him in the snoot!"

The voters, the sovereign citizens, many of whom didn't know George III from George V, ate it up. Capone, yes; King George, no.

Capone had taken to playing the horses in a big way. It was one game he never tried to muscle into: it would kill the fun if he knew which horse was fixed to win. The bookies loved him —over the course of the decade he dropped ten million dollars their way. Why not? There was more where that came from. Banks? He never entered a bank in his life, he proudly said; never had a bank account. At least not in his own name. As for the stock market, Capone was one of the three people in the U.S.A. who never played the market during the Twenties. "It's a racket!" he said.

The "Nickel Murders" next engaged the public interest in Chicagoland. (You had to hand it to the underworld, they always kept the citizenry entertained. This kept them from having to bother about civil rights, public health, efficient government, foreign policy, or other dull subjects.) Four mysterious murders took place in the spring and fall of '27. In each case the victim was a well-dressed man in tailored clothes, with expensive jewelry and a well-fitted wallet. In the cold right hand of each was a single nickel.

All four turned out to be from New York and environs—hoods, torpedoes, professional killers—hired to kill genial Al Capone. The liaison man was a recusant innkeeper by the lovely name of Dominic Cinderella, who tired of splitting his profits with the syndicate. He got the ice-pick-and-gunny-sack treatment. But the men behind Cinderella were the up-and-coming Aiello Gang, led by the brothers of the same name.

This gruesome twosome, Nick and Joey, were from the *Unione Sicilione*. How nice, they thought, if the Union could only be truly Sicilian—i.e., free from control of that crude Neapolitan, Alphonse Capone! Harking back to the methods of the Borgias, they offered the chef of the Little Italy Restaurant $10,000 to substitute prussic acid for some other ingredient in Al's soup. Professional pride affronted, the chef turned them down. With a sigh, they upped the ante to $50,000 and imported some talent, with the results as noted a bit earlier.

In order to cope with the new menace, Machine Gun Jack McGurn, Al's chief master-at-arms, had begun to put the boys through a stiff retraining course. It included gymnastics at the Capone private gym, but psychology wasn't ignored, either. "My guys have gotta have iron nerve," Al emphasized. "Make sure none of'm are, like, going to go cuckoo, Jack. Test'm out. You know what I mean?"

McGurn knew. "Going cuckoo" was an occupational hazard among full-time killers. Some of them began to get nervous, a sure sign of which was that they didn't button their collars or pull their ties tight. Once this symptom was displayed, the suspected man was taken around to visit at an apartment housing pretty tarts. If he recovered sufficiently to disport himself with credit, he was considered okay. If he didn't—the blooey-gun, the belly-gun, etc., etc.

"When a guy don't go for a broad," said Doctor Capone, "he's through."

The weeding-out process was just complete when word arrived from Capone agents in the enemy camp that the *Fratti* Aiello had tired of subtleties and were amassing enough dynamite to blow Al into the consistency of apple butter. The Capone men struck. Nicky Aiello was shot dead. Joey vanished.

"I'm going to take a nice, long vacation in the sun," Al said. "Then the coppers won't have to lay all the gang murders on me now. My wife and mother hear so much about what a terrible criminal I am it's getting too much for them, and I'm sick of it myself."

He took off for St. Petersburg and was told to scram. He removed to Nassau, where the Governor of the Bahamas threatened to invoke the Act of 34 and 35 Victoria c.70 against him, and—when he left rather than find out what the hell *that* was—warned the shipping lines not to bring him there again.

Governor Doyle E. Carlton wired the sixty-seven sheriffs of his State: "It is reported that Al Capone is on his way to Florida again. Arrest promptly if he comes your way and escort him to the State border. He can not remain in Florida. If you require assistance, call me."

But Judge Halstead L. Ritter issued an injunction restraining the sheriffs from "seizing, arresting, kidnaping, or abusing the plaintiff, Alphonse Capone." Al was so pleased that he began to talk about buying a place in Florida and settling down, like.

The year 1928 saw London, with three times Chicago's population, report eighteen murders and eleven executions (the other seven had committed suicide). New York City, with twice the population of Chicago, had two-hundred murders and seven executions. Chicago, "Hog butcher to the nation," rolled up a grand total of three-hundred sixty-seven murders, and no executions at all.

But Al, happy in the sun, wasn't worrying about statistics. He'd bought a walled fortress of an estate on Palm Island in Biscayne Bay, where he lolled on the beach with his wife and son. It had been a lot of fun furnishing the house, which cost $65,000. Al had personally picked out the linens, bedspreads, Chinese and

Persian rugs, and furniture. The favored color was canary.

Only once was the warm peace shattered. The neighbors alerted the Dade County cops that a war seemed in progress on Palm Island. It turned out to be a false alarm—Al and the boys were only shooting their Tommy guns at pop bottles bobbing in the Bay.

Back in Chi, meanwhile, "Diamond Joe" Esposito, a popular politician, was suspected of heresy against the Capone cause. Moaned his wife, "He was so good to the Italian people, and this is what he got!" What he got, to be precise, was fifty-eight poisoned slugs, which he failed to survive. Open warfare flared again. Senator Norris urged the President to "take the U.S. Marines out of Nicaragua and send them to Chicago." And a minister who denounced Capone from the pulpit found that eight insurance companies refused to issue policies for his church.

By September 8, 1928, things were so bad that Father Luis Giambatisti tacked a sign in Italian on the door of his church, San Filippo Benizi. Translation:

"BROTHERS! FOR THE HONOR YOU OWE TO GOD, FOR THE RESPECT OF YOUR AMERICAN COUNTRY AND HUMANITY — PRAY THAT THIS FEROCIOUS MANSLAUGHTER WHICH DISGRACES THE ITALIAN NAME BEFORE THE CIVILIZED WORLD MAY COME TO AN END."

The feud between Capone and Joey Aiello was killing his people by gunfire and destroying their property by bombings. At stake was the product of an estimated twenty-five-hundred alky stills run in the district. Capone's man was *Unione* prexy Lombardo. Late in September Lombardo took a dumdum bullet in his head. As not much head was left, identification was made by other means. One thousand families fled the district and holed up in small towns in Wisconsin and Michigan.

Al, unshaven, rushed back from Florida. He gave Lombardo a funeral of the traditional proportions: seventeen carloads of flowers, a brass band, a procession two miles long, and so on. But

Cardinal Mundelein refused to allow any more gangsters to be buried from church or to be interred in consecrated ground.

Lombardo's successor was Pasqualino Lolordo. On January 8, 1929, he welcomed three gents to his home and prepared a small party. Everybody ate and drank with gusto. In the kitchen, Mrs. L., preparing more sandwiches, heard someone say, "Here's to Pasqualino!" Patsy, who never read Emily Post, raised his own glass. Seven bullets missed him, but, as it happened, eleven others got him. Once more, Capone went unshaven.

To go back to 1928 for a moment: right next to Capone's island home in Miami was the island home of Secretary of Commerce Herbert Clark Hoover. The legend persists in Dade County that when Al Smith conceded defeat, someone suggested to Al that it might be a nice gesture if he were to go over and congratulate the President-Elect. Al is supposed to have answered cockily, "Why should I go to see Hoover? Let Hoover come to see me!" This—say the Dade County boys—is what undid him. Actually, presidential interest in undoing Capone preceded Hoover's election.

It had been earlier that year that Bob Lucas, U.S. Commissioner of the Internal Revenue, called one of his crack agents, Frank J. Wilson, on the phone. *"These orders come straight from the White House,"* he began. Then, "Frank, I want you to get Al Capone . . ." Frank said he'd sure try.

Capone, meanwhile, became convinced that Lolordo had been knocked off not by the Aiellos but by the Morans. Bugs and his buddies had begun to move into the dry-cleaning racket, in which Al had a large interest himself.

Bugs didn't go for the spotlight, as Al did. He moved furtively, was seldom seen by the general public. By now he had built up a new circle of supporters to replace those killed off in the gang wars. There were eight of them. Willie Marks was his bodyguard. Ted Newberry was his whiskey-peddler. Frank Gusenberg had done time in Leavenworth for making off with $400,000 worth of Post Office money; his brother Pete was a burglar and stick-up man. Jack May was a philoprogenitive (seven kids) safe-cracker.

Al Weinshank kept a shebeen. Jim Clark, Bugs' brother-in-law, was a bank-robber and crapshooter. Adam Heyer (alias Hayes, alias Snyder) owned the trucks that hauled the booze.

Seemingly out of place in this crummy crew was Doctor Rheinhardt H. Schwimmer, a fashionable young optometrist who had a taste for low company. "Doc" was also bored with fitting myopic dowagers with lorgnettes. He preferred to hang around the Moran headquarters in Heyer's truck garage at 2122 North Clark Street.

There were times when Capone, fat and paunchy as he now was, moved with the speed of a mamba to strike down his enemies. And there were times when he liked to hold back, to wait, to plot and plan, to relish his revenge in advance. This was also a characteristic of the late Joseph Visarionovitch Djugashvili, whose name in the rackets was Stalin. Stalin had just lately let a rival named Trotsky escape. Trotsky got all the way to Mexico before Joe lowered the boom.

Al had begun to feed Bugs "hijacked hooch" via a front man. This went on over a period of months, till Bugs looked on the "hijacker" as almost a partner. The night of February 13, 1929, the hijacker called and offered a load of popskull at $57 the case. Bugs agreed, asked him to deliver it to the garage at about ten-thirty the next morning. "The boys'll be here waiting," he said. "I'll have the dough ready," he said.

It was 18° above zero the next morning. A raw wind right off Lake Michigan blew snow flurries up and down the city streets. In her house next to Heyer's garage, Mrs. Jeanette Landesman was cleaning house. Bugs and Ted Newberry were on their way, and the other seven were already in the garage, a one-story building forty feet wide and a hundred-fifty feet long. The men were dressed in the usual height of gangland fashion: silk shirts, silk ties, diamonds, spats, cologne, big rolls in their pockets. Underneath one of Heyer's trucks his big police dog growled at its chain. A light mid-morning snack of coffee and crackers was going on, eaten with care so as not to spot the clothes, when the gong of a police car was heard.

Two policemen carrying shotguns got out of the squad car and went into the garage. Moran and Newberry, hurrying to the rendezvous, noticed the car and stopped. "Stay over here till they go away," Bugs growled. "Who knows what the flatfeet want now."

The seven men in the garage were not surprised. The coppers were always engaging in phony "raids." At most it meant a trip to the precinct house and a wait for a lawyer and bail. They calmly surrendered their weapons and submitted to being lined up with faces to the wall, hands in air. Then two men in plain clothes stepped out of the car and walked into the garage. They carried Tommy guns.

At a given signal one of them opened fire, sweeping his weapon from right to left. At the same instant the other one wheeled the second gun from left to right. One aimed high, one aimed low. They raked their targets back and forth. The dog began to howl.

Next door, Mrs. Landesberg heard the noise and went to the window. She saw "two policemen" marching two men to the "squad car" at gunpoint. She didn't recognize the men being "arrested," and ran downstairs to see what had happened. The four men had driven off when she began to tug at the garage door.

Moran and Newberry hadn't waited. They were already gone.

The police and the reporters found six men lying on their backs, dead, their hats still on their heads. The head of one had been almost blown off. The seventh man, Frank Gusenberry, was still alive, his head resting on the seat of the chair to which he had crawled. The dog lunged at the end of its chain, barking frenziedly.

Gusenberry refused to say who had shot him and died in a few minutes. But Bugs Moran didn't have to be told. He was now a mob leader without a mob. "Only Capone kills that way," he said. Bugs was through, and he knew it.

The coroner counted at least fifty slugs in each, all between the ears and thighs. Clark and May had evidently still been wiggling, because each received an additional load of buckshot.

"SAINT VALENTINE'S DAY MASSACRE," screamed the papers.

Rumor flew around that one of the executioners was a brother of Pasqualino Lolordo, the slain *Mafiano*. If so, it was a condign revenge. Capone's ace torpedoes, Anselmi and Scalise, were also named. Machine Gun Jack McGurn was even arrested, but was shortly released.

And then the blow fell. Together with the latest *Unione* head, one Guinta, two members of the Capone inner circle conspired to dispose of the Big Fellow and rule as a triumvirate. Al was really shocked. Was there no such thing as honor?

"I can't believe it!" he cried. "Anselmi and Scalise? Can't be true!"

"It's true, Al," McGurn assured him. And so did the other members of his grand council: Frank "The Enforcer" Nitti, Greasy Thumb Guzik, Murray "The Camel" Humphries, Three-Fingered Jack White, Tony "Mops" Volpe, and Bomber Belcastro, his pineapple expert.

The three men were invited to one of the old Torrio road-houses in Indiana, to attend a banquet (Johnny Torrio himself had more-or-less retired). There they were wined and dined, then beaten half to death with sawed-off baseball bats, then shot.

Hot upon the discovery of the bodies a fresh rumor made the rounds of Chicago: "The Sicilians are *really* out for Al this time!" It was time for him to take another vacation—and not in Florida, either.

"I been trying for two years to get out, but once you're in the racket you're always in," Capone confided to the fascinated but somewhat puzzled Major Lemuel Schofield, Philadelphia's Director of Public Safety. "The parasites trail you wherever you go . . . you fear death every minute . . . you're afraid of the rats . . ."

Capone and Johnny Rio, who had saved his life the time of the Moran raid on Cicero, had been picked up in Philly for carrying concealed weapons. They pleaded guilty, expecting a nice, short, safe three months in jail. "If I could stay on Palm Island with my wife and boy," declared Al, "I'd be the happiest guy alive. I want peace! Live and let live. I'm tired of gang murders and gang shootings . . ."

He may well have been telling the truth. The defection of Anselmi and Scalise had shaken his nerves badly. He was, after all, only thirty years old, and it may have suddenly hit him that another forty years of life in a bulletproof sedan could be very dull.

Capone and Rio got a year's sentence. They served ten months of it, starting in May, in Eastern Penitentiary. "That was the first time in ten years that Al was really able to relax," a friend said, later. He read through Ludwig's *Life of Napoleon* and he had his tonsils out. And in Chicago, Wilson of the Revenuers was following Capone's fiscal train with a fine-tooth comb.

His job was to find "gross income in excess of $5,000"—the standard exemption at the time—"accruing to Capone in any one year in which he had filed no tax return at all and/or any income exceeding the insignificant amounts he did report for other years." As Capone did all his business through front men and/or front men of front men, Wilson just wasn't finding.

Then someone told him about Alfred J. ("Jake") Lingle, "Mayor of the Loop," the *Tribune* reporter who was known to be close to Capone. So Wilson went over to see the august Colonel McCormick, publisher of the *Tribune*, and told him that the United States Government would appreciate Lingle's help. "I'll get Lingle to go all the way with you," the Colonel said, generously. And he sent word to Lingle to meet Wilson the day after next.

That area of America's second city where the elevated makes its loop was the richest booze and gambling territory in Chicago. Here were the theaters, posh hotels, plush night clubs. Here beer cost $5 a barrel more than in the rest of Chicago. Jake Lingle, unofficial mayor, was thirty-eight years old and had two children. A fellow reporter on the *Trib* described his "round, beaming, full moonish face . . . grin . . . cigar . . . cleft chin, curly hair; dark, rosy cheeks, medium height, thick and solid built . . . eyes . . . bland . . . cryptic . . . tired . . ."

And well might they be. He had been living a double life for ten years, since the time Al Capone came to the Four Deuces and the two men first met. Lingle knew every cop in the Chicago area, and he knew the Loop like his own palm. In a very little time he found his own niche. It was as liaison man between underworld and overworld in the strange climate of the Twenties, when the Law became criminal, and Crime became a law unto itself.

By 1930 Lingle—with an official income of $60 a week as *Trib* leg-man—owned a country home and a chauffeur-driven Lincoln, wore diamonds, was a big plunger at race track and stock market.

By 1930, Lingle's newspaper estimated, Chicago had ten-thousand speakeasies, each averaging six barrels of beer a week, producing a take to the syndicate of $3,500,000; each taking an average of two cases of booze a week to the tune of $1,800,000 a week for the syndicate. There were two-thousand "books" for betting, plus prostitution and the rackets, which paid tribute to the tune of $6,200,000 weekly.

By 1930 the City of Chicago was all but bankrupt, the public employees were unpaid, there was no coal to heat the schools.

Ex-Internal Revenuer Pat Roche said, "A one-legged Prohibition agent on a bicycle could clean up the Loop in an hour—if he were honest." And ex-Police Chief Collins summed up the complete breakdown of police morale: "The men who took money from bootleggers for overlooking violations of the Volstead Act were incapacitated from arresting them for any other crime. They had to stand for murder, robbery, and many other crimes."

Such was the atmosphere that Jake Lingle had helped create, and in which he flourished. And now the Feds were onto him. How well could he withstand pressure? Or had he already quit withstanding it? Lingle knew *everybody's* business . . .

And so, at noon of June 12th, 1930, a day before he was due to meet Wilson of the Revenue, six men (one of them disguised as a priest) came up to Lingle in the subway of the Illinois Central Railroad; and while five clustered around him the sixth shot him through the back of the neck with a stubby .38 revolver.

The ripples spread. Jake Zuta, of the Northside Mob, fled the town. The town caught up to him at a mechanical piano in a small Minnesota town. Lingle knew Al's business, Zuta knew Lingle's business . . . enter five men, single file: one submachine gun, one rifle, two sawed-off shotguns, one pistol. All five weapons opened fire. Total: forty-five slugs in Zuta. Another potential leak had been plugged.

Meanwhile Frank Wilson continued to hit the books. Capone had been spending $1,000 a week on banquets, drove a sixteen-cylinder limousine, wore $50 French pajamas, ordered fifteen suits at a time at $135 each. His private army had seven-hundred-fifty men on its payroll. And Wilson *still* had no proof that The Big Fellow received an income of over $5,000 a year!

In two years' intense investigation he had come up with nothing.

But his associates in the Revenue said of him, "Wilson sweats ice water . . . He never gives up." And so it happened one night when he was prowling around the crummy old Internal Revenue offices in Chicago that he blew the dust off of "three black ledgers with red corners." He didn't know it at the moment, but they were the books of The Ship, the Cicero gambling joint raided in the furor following the murder of Al Capone's ancient enemy, Assistant State's Attorney William McSwiggin. It was as if the dead man reached from the grave to strike.

A quick glance at the ledgers showed Wilson that The Ship had taken in over a half-million dollars in eighteen months from such divertissements as "Bird Cage," "Craps," "Faro," and so on. There was only one man in Chicago big enough to run an operation that size: it *had* to be Capone!

And, so far did his ears extend, Capone heard. He knew better than to try to bribe Wilson. Instead, he put a reward of $25,000 on Wilson's head. Wilson shifted his residence, kept on trying to trace the handwriting in the ledgers. He finally discovered it belonged to a gambling bookkeeper named Lou Shumway, then at the bowwow tracks in Florida. And there he headed.

Shumway turned out to be a mousy little man, and when Wilson told him, coldly, "I am investigating the income-tax indebtedness of one Alphonse Capone," Shumway started to shake till the change jingled in his jeans. "If you refuse to cooperate," the rugged Revenuer went on, "I'll have you publicly served by name with a subpoena. What will Al do if he hears that?" Shumway said nothing. He just shook and turned green.

Promised protection, he finally agreed to talk, and was stashed away in California under day and night guard. The next step was to show that the money had actually reached Capone. Every recorded money transaction in Cicero was put under a microscope and examined by Wilson . . . Well, well, and *who* was this Mr. J. C. Dunbar who had dragged $300,000 in cash, in gunny sacks, into the State Bank and bought cashier's checks with it?

It turned out he was Fred Ries, Capone's link-man with The Ship. Ries was a hard-mouthed, beady-eyed bandit. Threats of jail or gang revenge only produced from him remarks like, "Blow," "Get lost," or—most commonly—"fuck you." But he did have his weakness, and it was a lulu. Ries was deathly afraid of "creeping, crawling things." The Feds filed him away in a crummy little jail in Danville, Illinois, which hadn't been cleaned or fumigated since the Lincoln-Douglas Debates. Between the mice, the rats, roaches, spiders, bedbugs, fleas, and ants, Ries was soon darting from one corner of his cell to another, emitting shrill little yips of terror.

After three days he was playing the ritual scene required in all prison movies where the guy grabs ahold of the bars and utters the classic words: *"Get me ouda here!"* Soon the government stenographer was taking down his every babbled word, and then they packed him and six Treasury agents off on a South American tour until needed.

So, at last, finally, in the summer of 1931, Al Capone stood indicted before a Federal court.

He wasn't unduly disturbed. "I fixed everything else," he assured his two triggermen, Fur Sammons and Phil D'Andrea (who had succeeded Anselmi and Scalise); "and I can fix this, too.

There ain't a thing that can't be fixed."

"That's the truth, Al," "That's right, Al," they assured him.

Wilson's undercover man, planted in the Capone gang, reported to him, "Frank, the fix is in! The Big Fellow has a complete list of the prospective jurors . . . His guys are handing out $1,000 bills, promising jobs, offices . . . using muscle, too! They divided the list up into groups of five and all their bought big shots have been put to work at fixing their quota—every prospective juror on the panel will either owe his soul to Capone, or he'll be scared to death . . . the trial will be over before it starts!" The prosecutors, U.S. Attorneys Johnson and Green, went red and white. Who had let the juridical cat out of the bag was something for later. For now—

They went to see Judge Wilkerson, before whom Al was to be tried. The judge, who looked like something carved on a totem pole by a gloomy Indian, listened in complete silence. Then, speaking as if the words were costing him $10.95 each, he said, "Bring your case into court as planned, gentlemen. Leave the rest to me."

Trial day saw the courthouse jammed. People moved up the steps and through the corridors inch by inch, over a crackling carpet of flash bulbs. Capone came into court confidently, resplendent in a new mustard-colored suit that didn't match his scar at all. Phil D'Andrea was at his right hand, hair greased flat to his skull, eyes darting around.

Judge Wilkerson entered, all rose, all sat. Black-robed and grey-faced, the judge swept the courtroom with a glance. Not a few half expected him to say, "Hanged by the neck until dead!" What he actually said was just as startling.

"Bailiff. Judge Edwards has another trial commencing today. Go to his courtroom and bring me his entire panel of jurors. Take my entire panel to Judge Edwards."

And that was all. Capone's mammoth task of trying to fix the jury had all been for nothing. As the "fixed" jury marched out and the fresh jury marched in, his moon face showed its stunned surprise. Before it could recover, cold, oyster-eyed Judge Wilkerson gestured to Phil D'Andrea. "Let that man stand up . . .

"Do I understand that you have had the effrontery to come armed into a Federal court? Bailiff, take his revolver and bullets."

D'Andrea still didn't realize that things had—suddenly, to be sure, but definitely—changed. He flashed a tiny, tinny badge and sneered, "Look, bud, I'm a Honorary Member of the Cicero Auxiliary Police and I'm entitled—"

"Six months for contempt of court," said Judge Wilkerson. D'Andrea's face, as they led him away, was that of a man who dreams. "We will now proceed . . ."

Capone turned up next day in Oxford grey, then dark blue, powder blue, pea green; with hats, socks, ties, and handkerchiefs to match. He listened with unmoved face as witnesses testified that his phone bill for three winters in Florida was $11,000, that he had received $80,000 via Western Union, that he paid $27 each for custom-made shirts (sleeve monograms extra) ordered by the two dozen, that he bespoke fifteen suits at a time at an average price of $250 each and ten pairs of shoes at $40 a pair, that one afternoon he had stepped into a Miami gem-shop and picked up thirty diamond belt buckles at $275 apiece.

Jake Lingle had been wearing one of them when he was killed. The only time Capone's face changed was when a most reluctant salesman testified that Al liked to wear silk undies next to his two-hundred-and-forty pounds of well-filled skin-colored silk. Capone blushed scarlet.

The trial lasted until the middle of October. Unemployed were selling apples. There were breadlines. The Depression was on the country and held it hard. The jury, which stayed out until eleven at night, finally reported its verdict. *Guilty!*

As Frank Wilson put it, "Reporters ran out of court. Lawyers ran. Mobsters ran. Everybody seemed to be running but Scarface Al Capone. He slumped forward as if a blackjack had hit him on the back of the neck. Only the previous February I stood by the rail at Hialeah and the man I had been stalking for nearly three years sat in a box with a jeweled moll on either side of him, smoking a long cigar, occasionally raising huge binoculars to his eyes, greeting a parade of fawning sycophants who came to shake his hand . . ."

Cost of the trial to the United States: $150,000.

Capone was fined $50,000 and sentenced to eleven years in prison. In May of 1932 he was moved from Cook County Jail to Atlanta Penitentiary, traveling in a sealed coach on the Dixie Flyer. En route he expressed several opinions to his guards. "All I did was to supply a popular demand." "Nobody's on the legit when it comes down to cases." "A man in this line of business has too much company." "I never saw nobody forced at gunpoint to gamble." And, over and over again: "They hung everything on me but the Chicago fire!"

In 1934 he was transferred to "The Rock"—Alcatraz, the island where the Golden Gate meets San Francisco Bay. No news reached the world of what he had to say about life in that grim pile. In 1939 his family paid $37,692 of his fine. In November the most famous prisoner in the United States was released ahead of time for good behavior. Total time served: seven years and six months.

He smiled amiably at the small crowd which greeted him as he walked out of prison, but there seemed something blank and unknowing about his smile. This was definitely not the old Al Capone, even making allowances for seven and a half years in stir. In plain fact, the man who walked free to rejoin his family was a zombie, and would have been a zombie (assuming no one had bumped him off meanwhile) if he'd never entered prison.

Some number of years before Al Capone had known the favors of a woman whose name has not been preserved. She left with him a small present as a token of her affection—a tiny microorganism known to science as *spirochaeta pallida*. All the years while Al Capone was murdering his way to the position of Big Fellow, Shah of Chicago, Boss of the Underworld, and so on, the little bug had been proliferating. It entered his bloodstream, his muscles, and, finally, his brain.

Al Capone was a victim of paresis, the dreaded final stage of syphilis.

He spent his last years in the sun on Palm Island with his family. He liked to chew gum, bat a handball around, and to play rummy. His family and friends generally saw to it that he won, but once someone absent-mindedly forgot. "Who's the wise guy?" snarled Al. "Tell the boys to take care of him!"

In 1948, the same year that Rep. Andrew Volstead (whose Prohibition Enforcement Act gave Al the means to power) died, Capone's body began to fall apart. Finally pneumonia set in. When word got around that the former Public Enemy Number One was dying, reporters set up a vigil at the gate of his home. Faithful brother Ralph Capone wouldn't let them in, but he brought them coffee and cake.

The Big Fellow, who was responsible for the murder of five-hundred of his fellow-men, died in his bed. Requiem mass was refused, but burial in consecrated ground was allowed. In melancholy contrast to the $10,000 coffin, ten-thousand mourners, and twenty-six cars of flowers for Dion O'Bannion; the $50,000 coffin, twenty-thousand mourners, and forty cars of flowers for *Maficano* Angelo Genna; Al's coffin cost under $2,000, less than forty turned out to mourn, and all the flowers could be held in the arms of a single man.

MIDWIFE TO MURDER

SHORTLY BEFORE FOUR in the morning of August 31, 1888, a man named George Cross spied what he thought was a tarpaulin lying in Bucks Row, a narrow lane in Whitechapel, East London. The tarp, as seen in the pre-dawn gloom, was half in the street and half on the narrow sidewalk. Cross was a teamster on his way to work, and although he naturally never said so, he probably thought he would pick the article up and take it to work with him. The principal of "Finders, Keepers" was the least of the moral laxities then prevalent in the East End of Britain's capital. To his surprise, Cross saw that the tarp was a woman's dress. The woman was still inside it. Cross sighed, prepared to leave. Public drunkenness is much rarer in London nowadays than in any large American city, but 70 years ago it was very common. The teamster had a kind heart and a second thought. "'Ere we go, missus," he said, bending over and taking her hand. She didn't move.

At that moment a man named Paul came down the lane and stopped as he came up to Cross. "What's this?" he asked; and answered his own question: "Too much gin and wallop. Want me to give you a 'and, matey?" The two men took her arms and tugged. Then Paul said, "Oh, Lord!" in a sick tone, and let the limb drop. The woman's head lolled oddly. Blood dripped into her bosom and onto the pavement.

"She's warm," said Cross. "Maybe she's still alive."

"I'm getting to bloody 'ell out of here!" said Paul. The two men turned and ran to the corner of Bucks Row and Brady Street, almost full tilt into Police Constable Mizen.

"Woman dying!" cried Cross.

"She's dead!" Paul gasped. The bobby whistled and flashed his lamp—both signals for any other policeman within sight or sound. At once there was a flash in reply. The constable and two workmen hurried toward it.

Police Constable Neil had been walking his beat and had turned north into Bucks Row when he came across the woman lying in the gutter. He, too, tried to pull her up. And by the dim light of his hand-lamp he saw that her throat had been cut from ear to ear.

The body was still warm, the blood still flowing. She could have been dead only a few minutes.

Whoever had killed her had not fled north into Brady Street, or P. C. Mizen would have seen him. Nor had he made his escape south into either Bakers Row or Old Montague Street, or P. C. Neil would have seen him. Where, then, *had* he gone? The question was to be asked again and again as the late summer of 1888 wound to its close, and fear and terror of the unknown knifer fell hard upon the city.

Where did he go? Why did he do it? Who was he?

They are still good questions. After 74 years, they are still unanswered.

At that moment, though, the first concern of the two policemen was to send Cross off for a doctor. Or, rather, it was their second concern. First, they took Cross's name and address. Their third act was to send Paul to Whitechapel Police Station, a few blocks away. By the time Dr. Ralph Llewellyn arrived a crowd had already gathered around the body like vultures. It was obvious at once that he could do nothing. The woman was dead. He had just begun to make a further examination when the crowd pressed and jostled so closely that he almost fell onto the body.

With a ripe Welsh oath, Llewellyn straightened up and snapped his bag shut. "You can take her to the workhouse," he said. "Call me if you need to—if you have to." Then he went home to snatch what sleep was available to a physician in a district overpopulated with swarming, sickly, violent poor. He was in bed for only a short time when they did call him.

The yellow light of the workhouse morgue shone upon a group of pale men whose eyes looked anywhere but at the sheet-covered body on the slab. In the silence the drip of blood was plainly heard. One of the policemen was violently sick at the sink. As Dr. Llewellyn hurried in, a man came up and introduced himself as Inspector Spratley. Without a further word he then pulled back the sheet as far as the thighs. Dr. Llewellyn drew in his breath with a hissing noise.

The woman had been—literally—dissected.

Although these killings are frequently called "The White-chapel Murders," in point of fact most of them took place in the adjoining parish of Spitalfields. It was a matter of indifference, though, to most of the residents, in which parish they lived. Few of them ever went to church. Leonard Matters, a former news-paper editor who wrote one of the standard books on the subject of Jack the Ripper, had this to say about the vast slum which was the East End: ". . . the Jews, for the greater part, constitute the respectable members of the community . . . The most de-graded and hopeless denizens of the district are those whom, for want of a better description, one is forced to term 'Christians' . . . Squalor, dirt, drink, and general degradation seem to be the eter-nal characteristics of such an area." In short, Whitechapel and Spitalfields made up one vast Skid Row.

The neighborhood might be compared to a beach which the human wreckage of the British Isles was cast upon like a loath-some tide. The houses, none of which had bathing facilities or indoor toilets, were brick, long since blackened by the filthy coal smoke pouring from millions of chimneys; few of them were over two stories high. A maze of narrow alleys, lanes, passages, and courts housed this wretched population, a good portion of which was lodged in flophouses of the worst sort. And at night, in the dim, yellow gaslight, there crept out to practice their ancient profession an army of ancient prostitutes, battered vet-erans of the wars of lust.

Mayhew, an authority on the London underworld, called them ". . . those degraded creatures, utterly lost to all sense of shame, who . . . consent to any species of humiliation for the sake of acquiring a few shillings." He went on to say, "These women are well known to give themselves up to disgusting practices, that are alone gratifying to men of morbid and diseased imaginations. They are old, unsound [i.e., diseased], and by their appearance utterly incapacitated from practising their profession where [bright lights] would expose the defects in their personal appearance, and the shabbiness of their ancient and dilapidated attire."

Men of morbid and diseased imaginations! No better description of Jack the Ripper has ever been written! And it was upon this class of women that his crimes were committed.

Victorian England loved to believe, with delighted horror, that all whores had begun their careers as seduced virgins of good family. As a matter of fact, many of them were married women who did not turn to prostitution until they were past 30 years of age. The inquest into the Bucks Row case called a machinist named William Nichols to testify. Did he know the Deceased? "She was my wife," he said. "We 'ave—we 'ad—five children. Been separated eight years, cos why, cos she couldn't leave the booze alone, is why. But I forgives 'er what she done to me, now I finds 'er like this."

Coroner Wynne Baxter observed, "It is pretty clear that she had been living an intemperate, irregular, and vicious life, mostly in the common lodging-houses of the neighborhood." And bit by bit, testimony revealed the manner in which Mary Ann Nichols, poor drab, had passed the last few hours of her lousy life. One of her class had remarked to Mayhew that "life is as sweet to the whore as it is to the hempress." That last night was sweeter to Mary Ann than some because she'd had enough money to get drunk on.

At 1:30 she staggered into her flophouse and was accosted by the "Guvner," who demanded his rent. Mary Ann hiccupped. "I 'aven't got it. But I'll go and get it. Don't let my doss [bed]—I'll soon be back wif the money—look what a jolly bonnet I've got on!" She leered drunkenly as if to show that, newly bonneted, she would have no trouble luring a customer, and lurched off into the night.

An hour later, another old whore by the name of Mrs. Holland saw her staggering down Whitechapel Road. "Come 'ome along of me," the kindhearted Holland begged. Nichols shook her head. "I've 'ad me doss-money three times today," she said, "and spent it each time. But now I'm going to get it again." And she went looping away. Three-quarters of a mile and an hour and a quarter more, and Mary Ann Nichols had earned her husband's forgiveness. She was dead. The window above her body opened into the room of a Mrs. Green, "a light sleeper." The window opposite, across the narrow lane, was that of Mrs. Purkiss, who was not asleep at all. Neither had seen nor heard any noise at all.

"How could the deceased have been murdered without a sound, or any sign of a struggle?" wondered Coroner Baxter. "How could the killer have escaped detection?—for surely there must have been blood upon his clothes and hands. Unless—" an idea occurred to him. "Unless the presence of so many slaughterhouses in the neighborhood would make the people familiar with such a sight . . ."

The coroner's jury was adjourned until the 24th of September —it then being the 4th—but not until Coroner Wynne Baxter did some wondering aloud. "One is reminded," he said, "of the recent murder of Martha Tabram, who was found dead on August 7th, in Grove-Yard Whitechapel, with thirty-nine stab wounds in her body. She was a woman of the same class as Nichols. It was one of the most dreadful murders anyone could imagine. The man must have been a perfect savage to inflict such a number of wounds on a defenceless woman in such a way. One wonders if the two crimes may not be connected."

One is still wondering. It has never been established if Martha Tabram ought to be included among the Ripper's victims. For one thing, though she had been stabbed 39 times, she had not been ripped. Neither had her abdomen been opened and disemboweled, nor her throat cut. These were the trademarks of "*The Whitechapel Murders*."

Perhaps Jack was just warming up—getting his hand in, so to speak.

It will be observed that the name "Jack the Ripper" was not yet in use. That was to come later.

Still, it was enough to set the East End to shivering. And six days later, the East End was thrown into a turmoil by the discovery of another murder victim.

In the case of Martha Tabram, there is a story to the effect that a Mrs. Reeves, unable to sleep, woke her husband with whispers of nightmares and "nameless horrors" nearby. Until, just to prove how baseless her fears were, he went downstairs. There he found Martha Tabram dead of stab wounds. True? Maybe. But the night of September 7th, the day following Mary Ann Nichols's pauper funeral, if any nightmares were dreamt, people were afraid to go and look. Which was, presumably, just dandy by the nameless killer.

Because on the night of September 7th, he picked up a drab by the name of Annie Chapman, took her into the backyard of 29 Hanbury Street (a few blocks from Bucks Row), choked her, cut her throat so savagely with two slashes that her head almost came off, and then disemboweled her. He also removed what the accounts of the day delicately called "a certain organ." There is no longer any need for such squeamishness. The organ in question was the uterus, or womb.

Note the steady progression in technique. Martha Tabram is stabbed repeatedly, but her body is not opened. Mary Ann Nichols has her throat cut and is disemboweled, but nothing is taken. Annie Chapman's throat is cut, her abdomen is dissected, and her womb removed.

The slayer didn't stop there, either. And note the elements all the murders had in common—which all were to have in common: All took place within less than a square mile in the East End. All occurred in the early hours of the morning. All involved the use of fearfully sharp knives, all resulted in extreme blood-shed. And all the victims were prostitutes.

In no case, so far, did anyone hear anything. It is open to doubt that anyone did in any subsequent case, either. In silence the killer came, in silence he killed, in silence he did his bloody dissecting, and in silence he made his escapes through the mists and fogs which hung over the filthy maze of crooked lanes like a concealing curtain.

Whitechapel and Spitalfieids went mad with fear. Locksmiths and carpenters toured the district, reinforcing doors, installing bolts and bars. So far, though, the harlot-slayer had yet to enter a house and take a victim. When he did, the locks were not to deter him. But that lay in the future.

While the coroner's jury was still "sitting" in the case of Annie Chapman, the jury in Mary Ann Nichols's case reconvened. Dr. Llewellyn, harking back to the case of Martha Tabram, said it appeared that *two* knives might have been used to kill her. "Perhaps the killer was ambidextrous," he said. As for the deaths of Nichols and Chapman, the dissecting in each case showed that whoever had done them was no bungling slasher, but had *possessed considerable anatomical knowledge.*

"Have you any idea why nothing was taken from Nichols's body?" he was asked.

"The wretch might have been disturbed before he accomplished his object," said the doctor. "Nichols was killed in the open street, Chapman in a back yard."

"The ah, *organ* which was abstracted—is it easy to find? Is it large?"

"Not at all easy to find. *A man would have to know exactly what he was looking for.* How large is it? Hmm . . ." The Welshman paused to meditate, then came up with what is probably the *damnedest* comment on a woman's womb ever made.

"No," he said. "Not large—it might be fitted into a common *breakfast cup!*"

While police and public were furiously nominating likely candidates for the Rippership, it is surprising no one named Llewellyn. He sure had some odd ideas.

The coroner said, "There were no useless cuts . . . No mere slaughterer of animals could have carried out these operations. *It must have been someone accustomed to the post-mortem room.*"

There was another feature the Chapman case had in common with that of Nichols. Chapman, too, had been turned away from her doss-house for not having the fourpence rent. Her comment to the "Guvner" was almost identical with Nichols' to hers: "Don't rent my bed. I'll be back soon with the money. See my pretty bonnet?" Both women had only one way of getting money, by selling their withering charms to the not overparticular men of the district at sixpence a go. Chapman, being five years older than Nichols, may have been willing to accept only the fourpence she needed. But—this bit about the bonnets—did the killer make each woman a present of a bonnet, say, during the evening, so that they would know him and be favorably inclined to follow him into dark corners during the small hours?

No one knows, but the bonnet element will appear again.

There is only one thing more to say about poor Annie Chapman: Had she not been murdered, she would likely have died of malnutrition. She was that ill-fed.

Soon rumors flew about the terror-stricken East End, and, in fact, all over London. It was said that "an American" had offered the Sub-Curator of the Pathological Museum 20 pounds apiece for human wombs, and that a similar series of murders had occurred a few years back in Texas. An American tourist, acting under the same curious compulsions that makes American tourists so unloved abroad even today, got into a quarrel with a prostitute and was almost lynched. Then word got around that the killer was a man called "Leather Apron," who had a collection of knives and had threatened streetwalkers. He turned out to be a halfwitted shoemaker whose knives never cut anything worse than cow-hide, and who had shouted at a few sluts who had made fun of him.

The police picked up suspects right and left, and released them almost as fast. Whitechapel organized a Vigilance Committee to patrol streets as an aid to the police, who were widely denounced as incompetent. In plain fact, all was *not* well with the police or with Scotland Yard. The new Chief Commissioner was a retired general, Sir Charles Warren, who placed a great deal of emphasis on drill, spit and polish, and "putting down anarchist and republican agitation"—i.e., trade-union activity. He soon had managed to put down police and detective morale as well.

A red-bearded Irishman with a hair-trigger temper wrote a letter published in the *Daily Star* on September 24th, under the title, *Blood Money To Whitechapel*. It said, among other things, "If the habits of duchesses only admitted of their being lured into Whitechapel backyards, a single experiment in slaughterhouse anatomy on an aristocratic victim might fetch in a round half-million pounds [for social welfare] and save the necessity of sacrificing four women of the people!"

It was signed, *George Bernard Shaw.*

Sir Charles Warren bought a pack of bloodhounds and took them out for a trial run in open country. He acted the part of pursuee himself, huffing and puffing as he trotted off, expecting to hear the noise of baying any minute behind him. The hounds, alas, promptly took off for Tooting, in the opposite direction, and weren't found for hours! After which there was little more talk of bloodhounds.

Among the numerous foreigners in the East End was a woman known as "Long Liz." She was a tall woman in her forties, registered with the London Swedish Church as Elizabeth Gustafsdotter—or, Elizabeth, daughter of Gustaf, family names not being universal in Sweden at the time of her birth. She had married an Englishman by the name of Stride, bore him nine children, and was a happy, respectable housewife. That is, she had been until September 3, 1878, when the family went for an excursion aboard the *Princess Alice*, which was sunk in the Thames by a freighter. Over 500 were drowned—including two children of Elizabeth Stride, who were swept away before her eyes. After that she took to drink, left her family, and became one of the army of bedraggled streetwalkers who infested the slums.

When the panic set in, the majority of women living in the side-streets went in to their homes promptly as the lamplighter trotted past on his rounds, touching his long match to the dim and inadequate gas jets. But the majority of the drabs did not do so because they *could* not do so. The poor whores of 1888 had no rooms of their own—only frowsy fourpenny beds in dormitory flophouses like cattle barns. Therefore, it was only when darkness fell that they could ply their trade, going with their customers to the nearest dark court, alley, or yard. Fear or no fear, they had to go out on the streets to get the few wretched pence which meant bed and bread and—if they were lucky—a glass of straight gin or "a drain of pale" (brandy) with which to forget their misery.

Early Sunday morning, September 30th, a peddler named Diemshutz, who lived at 40 Berner Street, in the East End, was returning home with his horse and cart. Near the Elephant and Castle public house he was delayed by a fire engine which dashed by with its steam-pump shooting smoke and flames, the nostrils of the white horses flaring red as their hooves clattered on the cobblestones. Diemshutz had pulled up as soon as he heard the rhythmic shout of "*Hi! Hi! Hi!*" with which the firemen warned people aside. This brief delay was to cost the life of Long Liz.

At five minutes to one, Diemshutz drove up to the yard. His pony halted and refused to proceed. Next door, overlooking the yard, a socialist group was just winding up a party on the second floor. The peddler heard the singing as he looked into the yard, and saw, by the light of the club window, something—a sack, he thought—lying on the ground. It was actually Long Liz, still alive, who had just been choked into insensibility. Diemshutz did not go any further—fortunately for him, as the killer must at that very moment have been hiding behind the gate! Instead he went upstairs for a candle. No sooner had he done so than the killer swiftly darted out, cut the poor woman's throat from ear to ear; and walked away unseen into the street.

When Diemshutz came down with his candle the blood was still gushing from the victim's throat!

Denied the fullness of his cruel pleasure by this unexpected intrusion, the killer made his way toward Aldgate, farther west. Somewhere on his route he met a woman called Catherine Eddowes, who had just been released from the drunk tank at Bishopsgate Police Station. They headed toward Mitre Square, a deserted spot in a warehouse district. At 1:30, Police Constable Watkins passed through Mitre Square, shone his light all around it, saw nothing, and proceeded on his beat. At 1:45 he was back, shone his lamp again, and saw Catherine Eddowes lying on her back, her throat cut completely around, her face mutilated, and her abdomen laid open. She was, of course, dead.

Within a period of only 15 minutes the murderer had entered Mitre Court, strangled his victim, cut her throat, opened her viscera, removed her womb, removed her left kidney, slashed her face, nicked her eyelids, and made his departure.

Dr. Frederick Gordon Brown said, at the inquest on Catherine Eddowes, "The person who inflicted the wounds possessed a good deal of knowledge as to the position of the organs in the abdominal cavity and the way of removing them . . . The kidney is easily overlooked. It is covered with a membrane."

The police began arresting people right and left once more. To dispel rumors that a soldier had been the killer, the Governor of The Tower of London mustered his troops and inspected them and their gear for signs of blood; found none. The haughty *Times* of London had this to say, in ponderous prose: "The recurrence of these several murders at brief intervals of time, and with details more or less closely resembling one another, makes it more than likely that the two murders of Sunday morning will not be the last of their kind. There has been too much system and method and too obvious a brutal daring which cares little for the chance of detection."

In this the *Times* was 100 per cent correct.

And then came the letters.

Actually, the first communication had been received on September 27 by the Central News Agency—not Scotland Yard, as has been often stated. It may be that the writer believed that the police might not give it full publicity. It ran as follows:

"DEAR BOSS— I keep on hearing that the police have caught me, but they won't fix me just yet. I have laughed when they looked so clever and talk about being on the right track. The joke about Leather Apron gave me real fits. *I am down on whores and I shan't quit ripping them till I do get buckled.* Grand work that last job was. I gave the lady no time to squeal. How can they catch me now. I saved some of the proper stuff in a ginger beer bottle over the last job to write with, but it went thick like glue. Red ink is funny enough, ha ha. You will soon hear of me with my funny little games. The next job I do I shall clip the lady's ears off and send them to the police officers just for jolly. I love my work and want to start again. Keep this letter back till I do a bit more work, then give it out straight. [Central News Agency gave it to the police at once.] My knife is so nice and sharp I want to get to work right away if I get the chance. Good luck.
Yours truly,
JACK THE RIPPER
P.S.—Don't mind giving my trade name.
Wasn't good enough to post this before I got the red ink off my hands. Curse it, no luck yet. They say I'm a doctor now, ha ha."

The day after the murders of Stride and Eddowes, Central News received a postcard written in red ink and smeared with blood. It read:

"I was not codding, dear old Boss, when I gave you the tip. You'll hear about Saucy Jacky's work tomorrow. Double even this time. Number one squealed a bit; couldn't finish straight off. Had no time to get ears for police. Thanks for keeping last letter back till I got to work again.
Yours truly,
JACK THE RIPPER"

Not until this had the name "Jack the Ripper" been used to describe the killer. After this he was never called anything else.

It has never been proven that these or subsequent communications came from the actual criminal, but their tone fitted in absolutely with the public idea of the sort of guy the killer was—a cruel, sneering sadist, laughing at people and police alike.

The inhabitants of Whitechapel and Spitalfields held a mass meeting, which petitioned Queen Victoria to take extraordinary measures to safeguard the women of their communities. Fearing public outbreaks if something wasn't done, the Secretary of State for Home Affairs went to see the Queen in Windsor Palace, where she spent her days in her sitting-room—so runs the popular picture—in a black silk dress, with a white lace doily on her head. The results were as follows:

"Whereas, on September 30th, 1888, Elizabeth Stride and Catherine Eddowes were murdered by some person or persons unknown: the Secretary of State will advise the grant of Her Majesty's most gracious pardon to any accomplice, not actually being a person who contrived or actually committed the murder, who shall give such information and evidence as shall lead to the discovery and conviction of the person or persons who committed the murder.

Sir Charles Warren, the Commissioner of Police of the Metropolis, Metropolitan Police Office, 4 Whitehall Place, S.W., November 10th, 1888."

A more useless document than this, it would be hard to imagine. If ever there were a lone wolf in the history of crime, it must by this time have been obvious, it was Jack the Ripper. Doubtless the coppers had some qualms, too, because the publication of the notice was withheld. Meanwhile, another idea was given its head, and it doesn't seem a bad one. Excerpts from the letters to Central News were photographed, enlarged to huge size, and posted outside of every police station in Great Britain. The only thing wrong with the idea is that it didn't work. Not only did no one know the Ripper's real name or what he looked like or what he sounded like, it seemed that no one recognized his handwriting either.

The only result was the charge that the Ripper himself might have been a policeman!

And the cry continued, *"Resign, Sir Charles—Resign! Resign!"*

Meanwhile, someone had been doing a little pencil-work, and came up with the following table:

Mary Ann Nichols
  Murdered on August 31st
    Day: Friday
Annie Chapman
  Murdered on September 8th
    Day: Saturday
Elizabeth Stride and Catherine Eddowes
  Murdered on September 30th
    Day: Sunday

It was obvious that each killing had occurred on a weekend. There were a few possible explanations for this. One—which might fit in with the "jolly" tone of the Jack the Ripper letters— was that the killer had been amusing himself after a hard week's work. The other was that he was someone whose type of work took him into London only at weekends. Namely? Well . . . Was there a type of boat or ship which put into London late in the week and took off early the week immediately following? Well, there sure as hell was: and, in fact, there were a number of them, coming in on Thursday and leaving Monday, i.e., cattle boats.

Let us go back a moment to a question-and-answer bit in one of the inquests, the one on Catherine Eddowes.

City Solicitor: Would it require great skill and knowledge to remove a kidney?

Dr. F. G. Brown: It would require . . . knowledge as to its position . . .

City Solicitor: . . . likely to be possessed by one accustomed to cutting up animals?

Dr. Brown: Yes.

Now, a cattle-boat sailor is one thing and a slaughterhouse

butcher is another, but it was not impossible that there might be one person who had been the latter and was now the former—both jobs being, in a way, connected.

The police began arresting sailors. No evidence being forthcoming, they were all released.

On the afternoon of October 18, Mr. George Lusk, a respectable merchant who headed the Whitechapel Vigilance Committee, received what was probably the most horrible piece of mail ever to pass through Her Majesty's Posts. The small cardboard box contained an evil-smelling something-or-other, and the following letter:

"From hell. Mr. Lusk, Sir, I send you half the kidney I took from one woman, presarved it for you, tother piece I fried and ate it, was very nice. I may send you the bloody knif that took it out if you only wate while longer.

'Catch me if you can.' Mr. Lusk."

Dr. Openshaw, Pathological Curator of the London Hospital Museum, said it was half of a human kidney, all right: a "ginny" kidney from a heavy drinker, a woman of about 45 years old—and it had been removed within three weeks.

All of which tallied perfectly with Catherine Eddowes, whose left kidney had been removed in Mitre Square.

And so the stage was set for the last act of the drama of Jack the Ripper. Playing opposite him in this role was a woman 24 years old, said to be not bad-looking, but given to drink. As she was still young, she had been able to afford a room of her own; however, perhaps she had been neglecting business for boozing, because there was 30 shillings rent owing on her tiny room in Millers Court, Dorset Street, Spitalfields.

Five weeks had passed since the double murders, and the panic atmosphere had begun to subside somewhat. Certainly, on the night of November 8, Mary Jane Kelly showed no signs of alarm. She was thoroughly plastered, and was heard by her neighbors to be singing "Sweet Violets." In the early hours of the morning, the light of her fireplace was seen through the curtains by a neighbor, then it went out.

Did two of the other women living in Millers Court hear a woman's voice, in a low tone, say, "Oh, murder?" They said they did. And they said that they were always hearing such things. So they turned over and went to sleep.

About 9 the next morning police arrived on the double, alerted by the landlord, who had sent John Bowyer to collect Mrs. Kelly's rent. Bowyer, finding the door closed, had reached through a broken pane of glass, drawn the curtain, and seen Mary Jane Kelly lying naked on her back, body streaming with blood, with what appeared to be some "slices of meat" alongside her.

The police cordoned off the court, but didn't enter the room. Sir Charles Warren, bloodhounds still on the brain, had directed that—in case of another murder—nothing was to be touched till the dogs arrived. So the police sent word to the Chief Commissioner's office, and waited.

They waited all day.

No one notified them that Sir Charles Warren, knowing when he was licked, had resigned. Who was in charge, no one at Police Headquarters seemed to know.

Finally, Police Superintendent Arnold ordered the window frame removed (the door, it was at once seen, would not open because it had a piece of furniture wedged against it) and his men climbed into the room.

It might be stated right here that there is nothing to show that the Ripper had ever had sex with his victims immediately prior to killing them. It is true that Mary Jane had been stripped naked, but the nature of the deeds performed on her required that.

To begin with, the killer had cut her throat down to the backbone.

He had cut off her ears (as his card to Central News said he would do to his next victim) and her nose, and neatly laid them on the night table.

He had cut off both her breasts and laid them beside the ears and nose.

He had further slashed the face beyond recognition.

He had opened her abdomen from one end to the other.

He had removed her two kidneys and cut out her heart and put them on the table next to the breasts.

He had slashed her thighs to the bones.

He had removed her uterus and "the lower portion of the body."

He had removed her liver and placed it on the right thigh.

It was the last known murder of Jack the Ripper and it is obvious that Jack knew it and determined to close his career in a blaze of horror. The extent of his work may be further gauged by the efforts the surgical staff were put to in fixing up the corpse. In order to prepare it for identification, and to see to it that what was buried was a human body and not a mass of butcher's meat, four surgeons were assigned to restore—as best they might—all the severed parts. It took them *12 hours*!

In effect, that is the story of Jack the Ripper. Those are the facts known; all else is fiction. And there is a hell of a lot of "else"—that Jack the Ripper drowned himself in the Thames the following winter. That he escaped to America. That he escaped to Argentina. That he was caught and secretly confined in a lunatic asylum. That . . .

Then there are the theories. He was a madman. He was a mad doctor, seeking revenge on harlots because his only son died of syphilis; the one he was really after was Kelly, he had to kill the others so they couldn't reveal his questions . . . Well, for one thing, Mary Kelly was only 24 when she was murdered, and it takes decades to die of syphilis.

However, there might be a germ of truth in this story. In 1888 it was very easy to get into medical school, as long as you could pay your fees. And the sawbone-students of the day had a rather deserved reputation for immorality and high-jinks. It is not impossible that a medical student, mentally unstable to begin with, became infected with a venereal disease, dropped out of school, wound up in the East End where he became familiar with its maze of alleys, making escape easy. His mental condition becoming worse, he may have decided to seek "revenge" on the poor trollops of the district.

There is one other theory which deserves consideration. William Stewart, a British artist, wrote a painstaking book which he called *Jack the Ripper, A New Theory*. In short, Stewart believes The Ripper was—a woman!

Stewart asks four questions:

"1. What sort of person could be out at night without exciting the suspicion of the household or neighbors, who were keyed up with suspicion on account of the mysterious crimes?

2. What sort of person, heavily bloodstained, could pass through the streets without exciting suspicion?

3. What sort of person could have the elementary anatomical knowledge which was evidenced by the mutilations, and the skill to perform them in such a way as to make some people think a doctor was responsible?

4. What sort of person could have risked being found by the dead body and yet have a complete and perfect alibi?"

To these very acute questions, Stewart maintains, there can be only one answer: "*A woman who was or who had been a midwife . . !*" When his questions are considered, one by one, the answers are almost startling in the way they fit.

1. Not one publicly known source, at the time of the Ripper Murders, suggested the slayer might be a woman. Neither police, civilians nor victims would have suspected a woman. And certainly a midwife could have gone about the streets of East London unquestioned, for everyone would assume she was called out on a case.

2. If anyone had noticed blood on her clothes, the natural inference would be that it had been lost by a patient during childbirth. Moreover, she could have worn a clean skirt underneath, and—by a rapid change around in some dark corner—hidden the bloody one under the mass of petticoats worn by all women in

those days.

3. A midwife, trained in anatomy and physiology, would know as well as a doctor where the womb was.

4. Had she been found by the body of a victim, the easiest thing in the world would have been to say, "I saw her on the ground and thought she might have been in labor!" No policeman (or civilian) would have found any reason to doubt, let alone search her.

The next question to ask is, assuming the Ripper *was* a midwife or ex-midwife, *why* should she have committed the murders? Well, unscrupulous midwives, like unscrupulous doctors, have often practiced as abortionists. The women who hire them, overcome by well-earned guilt feelings, often denounce them afterwards to the law. Of such denunciations in England, Stewart says, "eighty-five [per cent] are made by married women." *And all the Ripper's victims were married women!* No abortionist ever admits to doing the dirty work for money—they are always "sorry for the poor girls!" Suppose Mesdames Nichols, Stride, Chapman, Eddowes, and Kelly had ever denounced, or threatened to denounce, such a woman for her illegal practice. Suppose the woman went to jail. Her grievance might have festered until it reached the point of mad blood-lust. At which point it found release in murder and mutilation.

Most skilled midwives, to take up another point, are ambidextrous. The coroner who held the inquest on Martha Tabram wondered out loud if her killer might not have been ambidextrous? It is a fearful picture: the killer, more cruel than any man against her own sex, strangling with one hand, stabbing with the other! And then, ignoring the torrents of blood, swiftly and silently cutting away with a knife in each hand!

Both Nichols and Chapman, it will be remembered, had spoken before their deaths of "new bonnets." Lures? Perhaps. For among the mass of burned clothing in Mary Kelly's fireplace was an item which all the neighbors agreed they had never seen her wear—a new bonnet!

One more thing about poor pretty young Kelly. The ruthless

knife of the Ripper revealed that she was pregnant! Perhaps the Ripper crept in through her window—but perhaps the desperate Kelly, abortion in mind, had invited in her own killer!

Two years later, in 1890, a Mrs. Hogg and her baby were found dead in the London streets, their throats cut from ear to ear. The murderer, who had wheeled the bodies a mile and a half in a baby-carriage, was a woman! Had this cruel Mrs. Pearcy ever been a midwife? No one thought to inquire. She was hanged.

So there you are. Into the mists and filthy fogs of London the Ripper vanished from public knowledge, exit made as abruptly and mysteriously as entrance. Butcher? Sailor? Police? Lunatic? Religious fanatic? Surgeon? Medical Student? Midwife?

One guess is as good as another. The only thing which can be said for certain is that for three months and a few days the largest city in the world lay trembling beneath the knife of a murderer who was infinitely clever, infinitely daring, and infinitely cruel; who said of himself, in his last communication to the press:

"I'm not a butcher, I'm not a Yid,
Nor yet a foreign skipper,
But just your own dear loving friend,
Yours truly—JACK THE RIPPER."

THE FORGOTTEN SOLDIER

SAM WOODFILL WAS A HOOSIER BOY, born across the Ohio River from Kentucky. His first recollection of hearing soldiering mentioned was one day when his maternal grandfather came visiting. The old man—a German immigrant and refugee from militarism—declared, "Ve vill haf no more vars!"

But white-bearded John Sam Woodfill didn't agree with his father-in-law. "I fought at Vera Cruz and the City of Mexico with Zachary Taylor—" he said, getting up to pat his First Sergeant's double-edged saber where it hung over the fireplace. "And I fought in '61 with the Fifth Indiana Volunteers—" here he took down his old Civil War muzzle-loader from the wall. "I had *my* fill of fighting," he said, "but I don't reckon the rest of the world has!"

Young Sam admired the saber, but the musket held his attention more. After that he paid less attention to his grandfather's claims for perpetual peace, and more to his father's tales of war.

Before long he had a weapon of his own and learned to use it, lugging rifle, caps, shot and powder-horn into the woods where squirrels abounded. The Woodfills and other settlers who had migrated from Kentucky to Jefferson County, Indiana, found their new home so much like the old that they gave the name of Indian Kentuck Creek to the stream along which Sam learned to shoot—and to make each shot count.

In many ways the rural and self-sufficient life of Sam's boyhood was a remnant of the 18th Century frontier. This particularly struck his biographer, Lowell Thomas (to whose book, *Woodfill of the Regulars*, the author is obliged for many details). "Woodfill represents a vanishing race," he wrote. "—an archaic type of American frontiersman, a real survival of an earlier day . . ." Thomas compared him to Daniel Boone and Kit Carson.

Old John Sam Woodfill went off to a G.A.R. reunion when young Sam was in his early teens, contracted pneumonia on the way back and died, age 72. The boy left school and went to lumbering with his brothers—but found it dull. So when the Spanish-American War broke out, he tried to enlist. He was under 18, and it never occurred to him to lie, so he was turned down.

But in somewhat over a year Sam had his chance again when the Philippine Insurrection broke out. Sam went down to Louisville, proved he was 18, was issued a blue woolen uniform—just the thing for the tropics—and sent off. His first experience in uniform was something less than heroic. He came down with the measles.

Stationed on the island of Leyte (where 45 years later American troops again landed—this time to drive out the Japanese invaders), the new soldier soon qualified with the rifle as marksman ($2 extra a month); sharpshooter ($3), and expert rifleman ($5)—even if he did goof somewhat his first time at the range by making his bull's-eye on another man's target.

Up and down the mountains and through the boondocks, the Insurrectos led the American troops a not-so-merry chase. And then the insurrection was over. General Aguinaldo and his men laid down their arms and took a level look at the chances for freedom under American supervision. In 1904, Sam Woodfill's Army hitch was up. He sailed back to the States and took part in a farewell winging in San Francisco's Barbary Coast. Then he headed for Indian Kentuck Creek to spend the rest of his life in the Peace and Quiet of the Hoosier State.

After three months of P. and Q., he was at the recruiting office, signing up again. In '99 the Army had given him a woolen suit and sent him to the tropics. This time, in view of his experience in the coconut country, the Army sent him to Alaska's Fort Egbert on the Yukon River north of the Arctic Circle. Sam liked Alaska fine, in all, he put in four hitches there.

Didn't time hang heavy on his hands in that lonely outpost in those pre-television, pre-U.S.O. show days? Not so you could notice it. As Woodfill explained it: "We would get a lot of extra ammunition from the supply sergeant and spend hours on the target range, doin' experimental firing. In this way I learned a lot about shootin' that I never knew before, including some little tricks of sighting and range finding. I was beginnin' to know just what I could do with a rifle . . ."

When the Royal Northwest Mounted Police at Dawson City, across the border, challenged Fort Egbert's hot-shots to a rifle shoot on the Fourth of July, Sam went along. The evening of the third saw an all-night dance, with liquor provided free by the generous redcoats. The next day the U.S. Army team was monumentally hung-over, while the Canadians were as fresh as so many daisies. Sam beat his opponent by one point. As for the rest of the contest, it was a case of The Maple Leaf Forever!

Losing most of his toenails to frostbite didn't sour Sam Woodfill on the Far North. He stalked and brought down wolves, he trailed bears and killed them, he scaled steep mountainsides to shoot goats and sheep.

The year 1912 saw him back in California again. After almost 13 years in the Army he had reached corporal's rank, but he took a drop down to private in order to be assigned to the Ninth Infantry in Fort Thomas, Kentucky, near his old home. In a short time he made sergeant.

Fortunately or unfortunately, Woodfill was a foot soldier. The second American invasion of Mexico (touched off by the second Mexican invasion of the United States) was chiefly a cavalry affair. Stationed along the Rio Grande from 1914 to 1917, Woodfill and his friends traded shots across the International Bridge at Laredo with Carranza's men. The rest of the time his shots were aimed at game that had four feet and game that had no feet at: all; i.e., deer and rattlesnakes.

When the United States declared war on Germany, Sergeant Woodfill said to his friend, Sergeant Weiler, "I've been practicing shooting all my life, and now it looks as though I'll have plenty of chance—"

"Hell!" interrupted Weiler. "What good's your damned rifle going to be in *this* war? The whole stunt in France is machine guns and artillery. Your rifle will be as out of date as a bow and arrow—"

"Buddy," said Sam Woodfill, softly, "the rifle is one weapon that's *never* going to be out of date! *Where there's a war, there's going to be rifle shooting!*"

The years have proved him right.

The old-timers like Woodfill, Weiler, and their regimental supply sergeant, Harry Blum, were soon informed that they were not, after all, going to be rushed to Europe. All over the country old non-coms were being given speeded-up officers' training courses followed by temporary commissions. Buck sergeants like Woodfill became second lieutenants, top-kicks became captains and old Harry Blum emerged at war's end as a full colonel.

Sam was shunted from San Antonio to Syracuse to Gettysburg, where—as acting captain—he was charged with organizing Company M of the 60th Infantry. The men came from all over the country, although Pennsylvania and New York predominated, and included five Indians. Ever since returning from Alaska, Woodfill had been engaged to a girl but had never felt able to afford marriage. Now, with a second looey's pay-packet, he popped the question and was married during a 10-day leave which terminated the day after Christmas.

Training continued at Camp Greene, North Carolina, all winter, in the course of which he received his commission as first lieutenant. In April, the 60th Infantry sailed.

The 60th's baptism of fire came on the Anould sector in the form of German .77 shells, which signalled their arrival with insane shrieks that shot through the brain like icepicks. Small wonder that the World War I name for what later became known as "combat fatigue" was "shell shock."

Legs were blown off, horse-drawn guns were hurled into the air like pinwheels, and shrapnel sprayed all about. A ghoulish note was added by Algerian and Senegalese soldiers whose favorite trick was to creep up on Boche sentries, slit their throats and carry off as souvenirs a nose, a pair of ears, a whole head, and —sometimes—more intimate parts of the anatomy.

Another new experience to the Americans was the plague of body lice, known as "cooties" or "seam squirrels." Lots of the folks back home thought that this was terribly funny; the soldiers, scratching frenziedly, would have been happy to share the joke (and the lice) with them.

Tempers began to fray and then crack. An Indian non-com in Company G, called "blanket-ass" once too often by a fellow-sergeant, shot him dead. As the outfit had just been ordered into the St. Mihiel drive, the angry Redskin was allowed to come along for the ride—his officers figuring that he might be killed in battle, saving a firing squad the trouble. The Indian, however, survived the entire war and drew a lesser penalty at court-martial.

In the Anould sector, Woodfill made the acquaintance of dugouts, trench warfare, flame throwers, poison gas and the potato-masher type of hand grenade. By this time, husky, freckle-faced Sam Woodfill was in permanent command of Company M, though he still was only "acting captain." The air of authority fitted the red-haired officer like a well-tailored uniform. Major Lee Davis was battalion commander and Colonel Frank Hawkins the regiment's C.O. In charge of the Fifth (Red Diamond) Division was General McMahon.

The St. Mihiel drive pressed forward. It was already known that Pershing and Foch had agreed that American participation would be limited to reducing the salient, that America's biggest punch was to be saved for the Meuse-Argonne offensive to follow.

When the really big push at St. Mihiel came, it lasted three days—just as long as the Battle of Gettysburg. A hundred-thousand Union troops drove back Lee; five and a half times as many U.S. troops drove back the Germans from St. Mihiel towards Metz, with *only* 7,000 casualties, less than one-third of the Union losses at Gettysburg. Fighting with the 5th were the 1st, 42nd, 89th and 90th divisions.

"I never heard such a roar of artillery before or since," was how Woodfill described the battle later. "There was incessant thundering . . . From the German lines came the roar of ten-thousand explosions. The sky flamed up as though the Northern Lights and one-thousand forest fires were putting on a show.

"Whenever there was a slight lull in the roar of the big guns, we could hear the staccato crash of countless machine guns. And through it all, the infantry kept marching up."

When the German resistance was smashed Woodfill's outfit slogged on foot to Malancourt, then to Liverdun and some intensive training. When he realized the semi-competence of the replacement drafts, Sam cut loose with some homely old Indian Kentuck Creek cusswords.

"These boys have been trained on the old Enfields," he exploded. "They hardly know what to do with these new Springfields! It'd be murder to send them up against seasoned German troops."

Although he did his best to whip the rookies into shape, he had his doubts how much good it did. As he put it, "We didn't win any victories in France because of superior training, [but] as a result of youth, pep, courage and . . . 'orders-be-damned' individual initiative . . ."

In a short time Woodfill himself was to display enough "individual initiative" to earn from no less than Black Jack Pershing (himself an old Philippine hand) the title of "the greatest soldier in the American Army."

"The purpose of the Meuse-Argonne offensive," wrote General Pershing a few days after the armistice, "was to draw the best German divisions to our front and to consume them."

On hand to carry out the consumption were 18 American divisions, though not all were in action throughout the 46 dreadful days of the battle. The Fifth, which was being reorganized, did not join the great attack until it was under way. General McMahon, who had been sent Stateside to aid in training and organizing fresh troops, had been succeeded at the front by Major General Hanson Ely. At the head of Woodfill's brigade was Brigadier General J. C. (Uncle Joe) Castner.

The Fifth moved forward at night to avoid being spotted by enemy observation balloons. Sam Woodfill described the nightmarish country through which they slogged as "ruined villages, forests blown to kindling wood, fresh shell craters, mud and rain, rain, rain. The woods were simply covered with rotting horses; dead men; human hands and feet, shoes half-filled with flesh and bones, blood, mud, filth, and stench."

The 319th Infantry was engaging the Germans ahead, and Woodfill's outfit hoped to slip across open country (and thus avoid the longer way through the woods) without being seen. But enemy machine gunners, covering their army's retreat, saw them soon enough.

When the Spandaus opened up everybody dived for cover. The best Sam could manage was a shallow ditch which protected his body, but left his pack sticking out. A stream of bullets poured into it, and then, to make the worst worse, the .77s started lobbing shells into the field.

Feeling that the end was just minutes away, Woodfill took from his wallet the picture of his wife in her wedding dress. On the back of it he wrote in pencil; "*October 10, 1918. In case of Accident or Death. It is my last and fondest desire that the finder shall please do me a last, and ever-lasting favor to please forward this picture to my Darling Wife. And tell her that I have fallen on the field of Honor, and departed to a better land which knows no sorrow and feels no pain. I will prepair a place and will be waiting at the Golden Gate of Heaven for the arrival of my Darling Blossom. The address Mrs. Samuel Woodfill, 167 Alexandria Pike, Fort Thomas Kentucky.*"

But then a long, strange silence informed him that shelling and machine-gunning alike had ceased. The 319th had mopped up the enemy resistance in that neighborhood. The next day they were shelled again. And the day after that was the one that made Woodfill famous—for a while.

The ridged hills where the Meuse River flows by the Argonne Forest were the buttresses of the *Kriemhilde Stellung*—Kriemhilde being the sister of Siegfried, and *stellung* meaning station or line—the massively defended German line of resistance. One of these hills was Cunel, toward which Woodfill's battalion had been cautiously moving when they were spotted. Just the day before, the Third Division had penetrated Cunel four times, only to be driven back four times by murderous fire from the Boise de la Pultiére.

On October 12, "elements of the Fifth Division" were to have a crack at it, and the fire from the *bois* was still murderous—as the Third Battalion of the 60th Infantry was in position to testify. Old John Sam Woodfill would have recognized the terrain. It was like that on which the Battle of the Wilderness was fought in 1864, tangled woods and underbrush. And just as the Confederacy had begun to crack behind the lines by the time of the Civil War battle, so had Germany begun to give way behind its lines.

Only five months before, German morale had been high. The Marne had been reached again, Paris was being bombarded, the French government was packing its records to ship them to Bordeaux. But a lot had happened since then. The Marne offensive had been stopped dead; so had the advance at Chateau-Thierry. Bourseches, Belleau Wood and Vaux were recaptured. At each blow from the Allied counter-offensives—Aisne, Marne, the Somme, Oise-Aisne, Ypres-Lys and St. Mihiel—Germany shook.

In 1916, Henry Ford had made his hopeless attempt to "get the boys out of the trenches by Christmas." But if this Meuse-Argonne campaign succeeded, the boys might well be out of the trenches by Christmas, 1918.

The front line darkness of the night of October 11-12 was dispelled constantly by the lights of star shells and by the blazing muzzles of thousands of artillery pieces. But nothing eased the cold rain falling in torrents on attackers and besieged alike.

Toward morning the downpour finally ceased, to be succeeded by a dense fog which wrapped the shattered Argonne Forest in a white blanket.

A total of 1,200,000 A.E.F. soldiers were engaged in a massive attempt to capture and destroy the great German supply line—the Sedan-Meziéres railroad—and the rich iron and steel area of Briey. Facing the A.E.F. was the German Fifth Army, whose commander-in-chief, Von der Marwitz, had ordered "unconquerable resistance!" The safety of the Fatherland, he warned his troops, was in their hands.

Shortly before six on the morning of the 12th, Major Davis, C.O. of the Third Battalion of the 60th Infantry, received his orders for the day. He summoned his officers to give them the word.

"Zero hour, Major?"

Davis nodded. "Over the top at six sharp," he said, "for the battalion and machine gun company."

One of the looeys swore softly. The noise of battle had died down a bit. "And take on the whole Kraut Army?" the looey asked.

The major smiled faintly. "Not quite . . . those woods ahead there, see 'em? Called the Bois de la Pultiére. We're to make a combat reconnaissance of them via the railway line passing east of Cunel and locate the German line of resistance. All right—alert your men."

Lieutenant Sam Woodfill passed on the word to Sergeant Smith, who had a question of his own. "How come the Heinies stopped giving us everything they got, Lieutenant?"

"I reckon it's because this fog interferes with their long-range artillery observations," Woodfill answered. "All right, Sergeant, it's almost six. Have the men fix bayonets."

The sound of his order being repeated came back to him. "Rifles ready . . . advance in skirmish lines, 16 paces apart." And then it was six. A whistle sounded. The men started forward through the underbrush, toward the enemy, invisible in the fog. There was a dimly seen clearing up ahead. Just beyond it, according to the maps, lay a ravine through which ran the railroad tracks leading toward the Boise de la Pultiére.

For weeks, the Americans had battled their way across a weird, outer-space-like desolation. Four years of warfare had crisscrossed the front with trenches and barbed wire, riddled it with shell holes and mine craters. Scattered amidst wrecked military equipment were the bones of the dead, uprooted from their graves. As an added touch of horror, heavy rains had flooded streams and formed swamps where mustard gas still lingered like a miasma.

By now, however, the A.E.F. had fought through the worst of this and was pressing into territory the Germans had held since their original invasion. Ahead lay the famous *Kriemhilde Stellung* and beyond that the enemy's line of supply. If the first could be broken, the second could be cut, forcing Von der Marwitz into a broad retreat.

The semi-silence which greeted the Third Battalion skirmishes soon proved deceptive. As they advanced into the clearing, an enemy machine gun chattered. Lieutenant Woodfill, walking at Sergeant Smith's right, heard him grunt. He gave no reply to the officer's, "Are you hit?," walked three more paces and fell heavily. It took just one quick glance to see that he was dead.

And with that, all at once, the shells started landing. Six men dropped. Then more. Then more. Those who were not killed were bowled off their feet. At first the men advanced on their knees, pausing only to re-orient a young kid who had started shooting madly toward the American lines. But within minutes the frontal machine gun fire had them pinned down. To advance straight ahead meant murder. But before Woodfill could give orders to head either right or left, two more machine guns had opened up, one from each side. Advance and retreat were now equally impossible.

If the entire force was not to remain trapped until wiped out by shellfire, the men had to get out of range. And this meant that those machine gun nests had to be destroyed. Lacking the walkie-talkies of World War II, Woodfill was unable to communicate with other officers. It might be, he thought, as he hugged the soggy ground, that no one else realized they were being enfiladed from three directions. But *he* knew! So it was up to him to do something about it—and to do it fast.

Turning his head and gesturing as well as his prone position permitted, he directed the men behind him to stay put. He ran his eyes over the ground ahead. Somewhere in front of him— he couldn't see exactly where—was one machine gun emplacement. A second source of fire seemed to be located in a half-ruined stable off to the left. And about 250 yards to the right was the third one, in the tower of what had once been the village church.

The men at those three guns were holding up the whole Red Diamond Division. And, for all Woodfill knew, they might be holding up the whole damned Meuse-Argonne offensive!

Rising half to his knees, he took one quick look at the terrain ahead. Then he was off—bent over and zigzagging—across the clearing. All three gun emplacements opened fire at once. He could feel the heat of the bullets as they flew past his face. It was impossible to get across the clearing. It was impossible to go back.

He knew in a matter of seconds that he couldn't make it, and he dived into the first shell hole he came to. Now he was safe from anything except a direct hit. But once again he was pinned down by the men behind the machine guns.

As if to remind him of that fact, one of them opened up just then. Rapidly, Woodfill decided on his course of action: there was no sense in just lying there. He had three machine gun nests to deal with—one to the right, in the old church tower; one to the left, in the ruined stable, and one hidden up ahead. Well, he thought grimly, take the squirrels you can see first . . .

There was a small window near the roof of the ivy-covered church tower. The gunner was invisible, but he was there all right and rattling away, but not at Woodfill. Being careful not to make a single unnecessary move which might betray him, Sam got his rifle into position and sighted in on the window. How high up would the gunner be? Not higher than he'd have to be, that was for sure. He was just as interested in keeping covered as anyone else . . . Right about *there*, probably.

Sam raised the rifle a bit and started firing. He kept it up till the clip was empty. From the church-tower window there was no sound nor movement. The gunner or gunners might be dead. *Or* they might be just waiting for Woodfill to show himself. Well, that was a risk that had to be taken.

Now for the stable . . .

This partly-shattered building had no windows. The door wasn't facing Woodfill, either. From exactly where, then, was the firing coming? Keen eyes that had picked game out of a hundred hiding places surveyed the stable wall. *There*! At the end of the gable! A board had been pried out or had fallen away. Sam put in another cartridge clip, drew his bead. Just as he was about to squeeze, a burst of machine gun fire came from the hole near the gable. Sam let loose and the Spandau stopped abruptly.

Without waiting, Woodfill leaped out of the shell hole and raced for the next crater. The other gunners *must* be dead, he told himself, for no fire came from the sides now. But the bullets from up ahead were coming thick enough, he realized, as he dropped down to safety.

As soon as those bullets started raking another part of the field, he was up like a rabbit and, also like a rabbit, popped into the next hole. The exertion shouldn't have made him short of breath—but it had. Or was it something else. His throat hurt, and his nose, and his eyes began to smart and tear. Just like when he grated horseradish on the farm. And then the full meaning of the symptoms hit him: *mustard gas*!

Maybe there wasn't enough left clinging to that hole to choke him to death (although maybe there *was*, at that), but there might be enough to leave him with a pair of half-ruined lungs, to say nothing of the spreading, raw blisters mustard gas brought out on the body. Well, that was just another hazard of the chase.

One hand automatically reached for the gas mask at his side, then stopped. He began to cough, but he knew it would be impossible to use his rifle effectively while wearing the protective mask. No choice but to get out of that shell hole, and quick!

This time there were no more craters in sight, but there was still plenty of machine gun fire. Sam took a reading on a thistle bush and hit the deck behind it. Then he waited, as before, for the enemy's arc of fire to shift. When it did he began inching his way ahead on his belly. Around a small rise, along a path, up behind a gravel heap. He crawled up the heap like a snake and cautiously peered over the top.

There was a patch of shrubbery about 40 feet in front of him. He thought he might head for that. But caution, bred into him from the time he was a one-gallus country boy hunting squirrels with an old muzzle-loader, held him back. Desperately he tried to focus his bleary eyes. He *knew*, by some extra sense, that something was wrong up ahead. And then he saw the muzzle of a Spandau thrust a few inches out of the bushes.

Woodfill tried another old hunting trick. He looked a bit past the spot he was trying to focus on and saw the gunner himself. He fired and the man dropped. He was pulled out of the way and a second German raised his hands to the heavy gun. Woodfill fired again, and the relief man dropped too. A third jumped up and then a fourth. Woodfill shot each of them through the head.

The fifth man in the machine gun squad had had enough. But instead of surrendering he tried to creep off. Woodfill cut him down. He'd had five bullets in his clip. And he'd killed five men.

There wasn't time to reload, and Woodfill had known there wouldn't be. His officer's automatic pistol was there on the gravel where he had placed it before commencing to fire. A sixth German sprang toward him out of nowhere, and Woodfill got him with the automatic. Then he waited. The mist had begun to lift. Everything was quiet. He put a fresh clip into his rifle and started forward.

Six dead men in field-gray uniforms lay sprawled around the machine gun with no tops to their heads. Woodfill hoped his own men were coming up behind him. He kept on. There was another dead man in his path. But his swift-thinking hunter's mind went taut at the idea of a seventh dead man. He'd fired only six shots. At that second the "dead man" leaped to his feet, seized Woodfill's rifle, tossed it away and reached for his own Luger.

Woodfill didn't have to reach. The automatic was still in his hand and he shot the *oberleutnant* through the heart. This time he stayed dead.

Woodfill thrust the German's Luger into his pocket. For the first time he turned his head and took a look behind. His men *were* coming up behind him! At least, some of them were. He signaled them to move forward. Now running, now creeping, now squatting, he made his way through the tangled underbrush. And all the while the Spandaus rattled and the shells screeched.

Woodfill sighted a fourth machine gun nest. He now realized they were spotted through the Bois de la Pultiére in a zigzag pattern so as to afford the maximum cover to the retreating German Fifth Army. This one was located in a dugout that wasn't quite deep enough. What followed was a repetition of the last turkey shoot. One by one, Sam Woodfill picked off the five gunners.

He moved so softly that he was on top of three Germans carrying ammo before they knew it. When they did know it, and saw that they were covered, up went their hands. *"Kamerad, kamerad!"*

"Why, they're just kids!" Woodfill thought. He disarmed them and gestured them toward the American lines. Gunfire was coming from all around, now, and when it started shaving the bark off nearby trees, he took to his belly again. From behind gnarled tree-roots he looked down into a ravine. Some of his men were trying to get through it, but a machine gun (the fifth he had encountered) was raking the ground. Woodfill soon had it located and started crawling up on it.

The mud here was almost liquid, and there was a 30-foot stretch of it to cover before Woodfill could start to shoot. But once he started firing, he didn't stop until his clip was empty. It was almost a mathematical formula: *5 shells per clip + Sam X 5 Germans per gun-crew = 5 dead Germans.*

After dropping the fifth man at the fifth gun and seeing no one else move, Woodfill loped on ahead. When someone to the right started shooting at him, he jumped into a trench. The trench being there was a lucky break for Sam, but not for the German who was inching along the trench toward the machine gun. There was no space to raise a rifle, so the Hun lifted his pistol—and fell, a Colt bullet in his belly.

Then, hearing footfalls, Sam whirled. Around a bend in the trench came another of Von der Marwitz's "unconquerable resisters," rifle at the ready, bayonet thrusting. And at that moment Sam's automatic jammed.

Seizing a pickaxe someone had left sticking in the side of the trench, Woodfill brained the rifleman. It was almost without thinking that he whirled around again in time to see the German he had just shot leveling his Luger at him. Another blow of the pickaxe and another dead Hun.

Out of the trench again, Woodfill kept up a running fire at the Germans, who now seemed to be more and more out in the open. In a few minutes he found out why. *He was inside of the Kriemhilde Stellung itself, and surrounded by Germans!*

Well, didn't the Alaskan Indians and Eskimos creep into the middle of a caribou herd to do their most effective killing? The firing was so heavy, the enemy couldn't figure from what point Woodfill was sniping at them. Certainly they never thought he was inside their own lines!

But with the steady, relentless American advance, more and more of Sam's men came up until he was able to assemble some of them. Once more Lieutenant Woodfill was fighting as the head of an outfit, and no longer as a lone wolf. And just at that time it became impossible to do any more fighting. The German artillery stepped up its fire to cover the retreat of the front-line Hun troops, and what there was left of Woodfill's company began to dig in hastily.

But, it rapidly became clear, there was no cover from that murderous fire. Once communications were re-established,

Major Davis ordered a withdrawal, especially since no supporting troops had moved in behind Woodfill and his men. Once again the skirmishers were pinned down in shell holes . . . Had it all been for nothing? Then, suddenly, in the late afternoon, the enemy barrage ended.

The next two days brought the capture of the Bois de la Pultiére and of Cunel by the Fifth Division, which suffered terrible casualties in the attack. But Woodfill was no longer with his men. The cold and rain had been too much for him, and the battalion surgeon had ordered him evacuated to forestall possible pneumonia. Before Sam quite knew what was happening, he found himself at the base hospital all the way back in Bordeaux. Here the staff did some poking and probing and decided he needed an immediate operation. While he was recovering, the armistice was signed.

When he got on his feet again, Woodfill was put in charge of the delousing detail at the Bordeaux port of embarkation. It was during this tour of duty that Sam received the Congressional Medal of Honor from General Pershing, who referred to him as "the out-standing soldier of the A.E.F.—in fact, the greatest soldier in the American Army."

High praise, indeed. But did it make up for the fact that the mustard gas of that morning in the shell-torn Bois de la Pultiéres had affected his eyes to the degree that he could no longer maintain his former marksmanship standard? Woodfill never said.

Others honors came his way, too. Promotion to captain; the Croix de Guerre with palm, pinned on him by his divisional C.O., General Ely; the Legion of Honor, together with two whiskery kisses by a French admiral. Both Italy and Montenegro decorated him. "An excellent man and a born soldier," the War Department wrote into his records.

Mustering-out time for Woodfill came at the end of 1919. But he couldn't quite see himself as a civilian—not yet, anyway. True, he and his wife had bought a small farm, but he lacked the capital to make it a paying proposition. His years overseas and in Alaska counted as double-time. If he could stay in the army until

1923, he could retire on full pension. Would the army let him re-enlist?

Yes, said the chair-borne colonels, picking their teeth . . . but not as a commissioned officer. They had more than enough to go around. So "the greatest soldier in the American Army" shipped over as a buck sergeant. His Medal of Honor plus a nickel entitled him to a ride on the subway.

Woodfill didn't complain. He was a Regular Army man and ob-scurity contented him. And obscure he remained until that mov-ing day in 1921 when the nation buried its Unknown Soldier at Arlington. It was decided that three veterans of the A.E.F. would be among the pallbearers. A committee selected 3,000 names and winnowed out 100.

The final choice was up to General Pershing. He selected Ser-geant Alvin York, Colonel Whittlesey of the Lost Battalion and Sergeant (formerly Captain) Samuel Woodfill. And once again Pershing commented. "That man was the outstanding soldier of the A.E.F."

This made the papers. Who was Woodfill? The public wanted to know, and the press told them. Woodfill met President War-ren G. Harding and ex-Presidents Taft and Wilson and Secretary of War John W. Weeks. He met Marshal Foch. Congress ad-journed in his honor. The Stock Exchange suspended business in tribute to him. The Senate and House of Representatives gave him a banquet. When he appeared at theaters he received stand-ing ovations and crowds thronged around him in the streets.

And then he went back to his duties at Fort Thomas, Ken-tucky, and the country forgot about him, and—for that matter —about Sergeant York and Colonel Whittlesey. It was briefly re-minded of the latter and of the four terrible days of the Lost Bat-talion when Whittlesey killed himself.

Woodfill's name too, reappeared in the papers, but under less grim circumstances. Since Sergeant Sam did not have the money to meet a note on the farm to which he hoped to retire, his C.O. gave him three months leave. He started to work as a day laborer, but when this became known the Keith Theaters (later RKO) raised $10,000, settled the mortgage and bought Woodfill an insurance policy.

He left the Army, he thought for good, in December, 1923, and settled down to plow the land he had left almost a quarter of a century before.

After years of peaceful retirement on his Indiana farm, Woodfill heard the drums of war beat once more. Immediately after the attack on Pearl Harbor, the aging veteran offered his services to his country again. His request was granted and on July 1,1942, he was called back to duty, and commissioned a major.

Despite his assurances to the contrary, the Army considered him too old to go overseas, and he was assigned to the Infantry Branch at Fort Monroe, Virginia. He was relieved of active duty in August, 1943. In 1948 he was granted permanent rank as major in the Army of the United States, Retired List.

He died on his farm near Madison, Indiana, on August 10, 1951, and was buried there. Later a second funeral, with full military honors, was held in the National Cemetery at Arlington, Virginia, and here the remains of the old hero lie.

THE DEATH OF THE HENRY CLAY

RED-HOT COALS fell hissing into the water, black smoke and yellow-orange sparks came roaring forth from two sets of double smokestacks. The Hudson River steamers looked like twins as they showed their long, clean lines, gleaming with gold leaf and white paint that morning of July 28, 1862. The great golden eagle fixed to the foremast of the *Henry Clay* showed her to be racing ahead of her sister ship, the steamboat *Armenia*, whose bare foremast was a few yards behind. Coal dust was powdering both vessels with a sooty film.

The humming vibrations of their steeple-engines caused the two craft to quiver and shake. Stephan Allen, the 84-year-old ex-mayor of New York City, pushed forward, his long white locks streaming in the wind behind him.

"What is the purpose of this infernal racing, sir?" he demanded of First Mate Dildo Stone, his still-deep voice quivering with indignation.

"The *Henry Clay's* the best boat on the River, Your Honor, and the *Armenia's* got to be made to know it!" Dildo Stone yelled above the noise. "We're going to rub Ike Smith's nose in it!" he crowed gleefully.

Stone didn't know that Captain Isaac Smith, the owner-skipper of the *Armenia*, was not aboard his vessel.

Cap'n Ike had stayed behind in Albany on business. The man in the *Armenia's* wheelhouse was her pilot, "Ik" Polhemius, an unusually stubborn Hudson River Valley Dutchman—and they were a stubborn breed! "Ik would rather go *through* a stone wall than go over it," they said in his native Tarrytown. And now, as he guided his vessel downriver, Polhemius had exactly one idea in his hard Hollander's head: to beat the *Henry Clay* into the Jay Street dock in New York City and prove to her Captain, John Tallman, whose boat was best.

What Pilot Polhemius didn't know was that Captain Jack was out cold in his cabin—some said with food poisoning, some said sleeping off a monumental drunk.

Both ships, each without the guiding hand of its captain, tore down the Hudson at top, engine-wracking speed.

Behind the Honorable Stephan Allen came the beautiful Mrs. Wadsworth.

"Oh, please, can't you stop this dangerous racing!" she begged.

"No danger at all, ma'am," said Dildo Stone, eyeing the widow's heaving bosom with approval.

Smooth-tongued riverboat gamblers offered to make book on the race. They proposed odds of two to one on the *Henry Clay*—but the loyal officers, who were the only ones interested, scoffed. They demanded at least three to one, or no bets.

"The good old 'Harry' could beat any boat afloat, with her starboard paddle broke!—Ain't that right, you black gang fellows?" they yelled across the wet mahogany bar.

The firemen, coming up in relays to take aboard some liquid fuel of their own, yelled profane approval and dipped their mustaches in the suds. "If the firemen are gonna stoke the furnaces, we gotta stoke the firemen!" whooped the second mate.

Dildo Stone stuck his head into the bar saloon, bellowed, "The *Armenia's* forged ahead two lengths! Are you going to let that garbage-scow beat us while you set here guzzling? Are you going to let a boat with a great Whig name be beat out by a bunch of Locofoco Democrats?"

Shouting and roaring defiance, the black gang ran for their furnace-room. Slowly but inexorably, the *Henry Clay* closed in on her rival, her officers and deck hands lining the starboard rails and screaming threats and curses. Aboard the *Armenia*, Pilot Ik Polhemius kept grimly to his course.

The two ships crept closer to one another.

"*Fen-ders!*" called First Mate Stone. A deck hand, his arms piled with anti-collision equipment, stood out on the starboard paddle box of the *Clay.* The ships were only a few feet apart; their prows seemed absolutely even. To the right lay Turkey Point. Kingston, the next landing, was five miles south. The engines thumped feverishly, the walking-beams flew up and down, the four paddle wheels beat the river to froth. On the top deck of the *Armenia* an unknown man suddenly appeared, brandishing a buffalo gun.

"Keep off, damn you!" he screamed. "Keep your distance, or I'll shoot!"

Polhemius suddenly headed the *Armenia* on a slanting course toward the west bank. A bedlam of furious shouts shot up from the other ship: "*She's going to try to cut us off! They mean to pass! Stop her!*"

The *Henry Clay's* veteran pilot, Jim Elmendorf, as stubborn a Valley Dutchman as Ik Polhemius, went red with fury. He spun his wheel with all his might. The *Clay*, minding the wheel instantly, leaped at top speed to starboard. With a shattering crash the *Henry Clay's* prow ripped and splintered into the port side of the *Armenia . . .*

On the morning of the race, July 28, 1852, the Albany, N.Y., newspapers as usual covered their front pages with classified ads. Like this one:

Steamboat *Armenia* for Hudson, Catskill, Kingston, Poughkeepsie, Newburgh, and New York City. Leaves Albany every morning at 7. Arrives at Jay St. dock, N.Y.C., at 4. No Sunday trip. Meals served aboard.

Or like this one:

The new and elegant steamer *Henry Clay* will leave Albany at 7 every morning for Hudson, Catskill, Kingston, Poughkeepsie, Newburgh, and New York City. Arrives at dock, foot of Jay St., at 4 p.m. N.B. UNDER NO CIRCUMSTANCES WILL ANY OF THE ABOVE LANDINGS BE OMITTED.

Among those who decided to take passage on the *Clay* were two relatives of the famous author, Nathaniel Hawthorne—his sister Maria and their Uncle Joe Dike, of Salem, Mass. With them was a friend, Dr. Jos Speed of Baltimore.

Uncle Joe, who had been traveling for his nerves, was reassured by the N.B. in the *Clay's* ad. "You see, Maria—they promise not to skip any landings," he said.

Maria asked what that meant, and was told that it was a more-or-less guarantee against racing. Rivalry between the riverboats was keen, and one of the favorite ways to gain time was to skip landings in between Albany, the State capital, and New York City. Ships were anxious to show their speed, too, because railroad competition was beginning to be felt.

Most travelers up and down the Hudson Valley still preferred, though, to take a cool voyage by water rather than one on the hot and dirty "trains of cars."

And one of the favorite boats was the *Henry Clay*.

She was 206 feet long and only two years old. The famous boat-builder, Tom Collyer, who owned the dockyards on 20th Street and the East River, had put her together for $38,000. He and several partners still owned her. As a matter of fact, in those same yards Collyer had built the *Armenia*, too, and sold her to Captain Isaac Smith. As both ships were of a size and had almost identical engine work and took the same routes, it was almost inevitable that they should race.

But racing could be dangerous—so Tom Collyer on behalf of his partners and Cap'n Ike Smith on behalf of himself had signed a compact, ". . . *herebye* binding ourselves, the masters, officers and crews of our vessels, that we and they shall not race nor allow to be raced, the river steamers *Henry Clay* and *Armenia*; and that furthermore . . ." Here they tossed a coin. It came up heads—Tom Collyer's choice. ". . . and that furthermore the

Henry Clay shall be the first to leave both Albany and New York City."

That settled *that*. Collyer was aboard this morning of July 28 and went up to have a word with Captain Jack Tallman in the latter's cabin. His knock was answered by Mrs. Tallman, a tall and bony woman of forbidding aspect. Mr. Collyer removed his beaver.

"Morning, ma'am. Captain Jack in his cabin?"

"Sick," said Mrs. Captain tersely.

"Dear me. Nothing serious, I hope?"

"Food p'isoning. Ett too many bad 'ysters. Doctor told me to medicate him with lobelia drops. I'm doin' it."

"I trust the trip will see him restored to health by evening," he said, nodded, and took his departure. First Mate Dildo Stone and Pilot Jim Elmendorf would have to manage without the captain. They'd done it before.

On the dock the "runners," or "barkers," were touting their ships at the top capacities of their leather lungs.

"*All aboard of the* ARMENIA! *Never had no accident, never had no fire!*"

"*Come all ye good citizens, take the* HENRY CLAY! *Assured with Stuyvesant's of New York for $50,000!*"

Fare was officially advertised at one dollar, but by 6:45 a.m. as late arrivals stood hesitating on the docks, the runners began to beat the price down—anything to fill up the ships.

"*The splendid* ARMENIA—*seventy-fi' cents!*" "*The glorious* HENRY CLAY—*sixty-fi' cents!*" In 10 minutes the price on each had gone down to a half dollar and the impatient touts seized hold of the bags of still-uncertain passengers and tossed them aboard—leaving the travelers to follow or (if they chose) to fight.

It was 6:59. Dildo Stone, showy and important in his blue and gold first mate's uniform, lined the Negro stewards, their white jackets gleaming with starch, along the rails. He took out his watch, began a countdown.

"*Cast-OFF!*" he yelled. The *Henry Clay*, with a toot of her whistle and a billow of smoke from each of her twin smokestacks, moved out of the docks. There were 300 passengers aboard.

And a split second later the *Armenia* followed her. Ik Pol-hemius was at the *Armenia's* wheel—and Ik hadn't signed any compact. "Full speed ahead!" he signaled his engine room. And —with a roar that could be heard in the old Statehouse—he shouted, "And I mean *full*-by-damn SPEED!"

No one was having a finer time than the group of men crowded at the stern. They had found rare fun—a lady to whom gentlemen didn't have to be polite! The girl couldn't have been over 18, and she wasn't bad to look at. But what had turned the crowd of men into something like a mob was her costume. Instead of hoop skirts and crinoline, modestly concealing her lower "limbs" (no lady in those days had *legs*!), the girl wore something resembling Turkish pantaloons.

"A Bloomer Girl!" the men shouted, gleefully. The young chit was a follower of Mrs. Amelia Bloomer, the Feminist leader. "Bloomers! Bloomers!"

"Hey, girlie," a fat hay-merchant yelled, "do you believe in free love and votes for women and all that stuff?"

The girl turned red; the mob hooted and catcalled, pressed closer. And then, suddenly, there was a man in between her and the others. A gambler, by the fancy look of him, ringed fingers fiddling with the ruffles on his shirt.

"All right, get on about your business—leave the young lady alone," he said. Everything was suddenly so quiet the beat of the steeple-engines was clearly heard. The crowd tensed, took a step forward.

"You stick to fleecing farmers, cardsharp!" someone yelled. And then, suddenly, the ringed fingers had produced a derringer from the ruffles flowing onto the embroidered vest. The mob went limp, fell back before the menace of the short-barreled, huge-bored little weapon.

"I shot numerous amounts of men in the Mexican War," said the two-card monte man, softly; "better than any I see here now." No one seemed disposed to dispute it. He turned to the girl in the weird costume. "Allow me to escort you to the Ladies'

Cabin, miss," he said. She hesitated, but—evidently deciding the moment was not ripe for a vindication of the rights of women —took his arm and walked through the suddenly-opened path through the crowd.

The *Clay* was easily ahead as the town of Hudson came near —but the happy cheers turned into shouts of rage as it became obvious that the *Armenia* was going to skip this landing. With a hoot of her whistle she headed out, instead, down the Athens Channel on the other side of the River. At the orders of First Mate Dildo Stone, the *Clay's* stop was fast and furious. Baggage was flung aboard—and passengers. But owner Thomas Collyer was moved to a mild protest to Pilot Jim Elmendorf as the latter's wife, seated in her rocking chair in the pilot house, calmly knitted.

"The compact, Captain Jim—"

Elmendorf's answer was brief and convincing. "*Armenia's* just broke the compact, Mister Collyer, by not landing. She needs to be taught a lesson."

Collyer said, "Hmm . . ."—and no more. He made an official protest, his duty was done. The faithless *Armenia* was a clear mile ahead as the *Clay* pulled out of Hudson and took the Channel with a bone in her teeth. The Athens Channel was dangerous water. Only seven years before, the steamboat *Swallow*, racing against the steamers *Empire* and *Rochester* on an April night, was wrecked on the Brig Noah's Rocks. She sank almost at once, drowning 60-odd of her passengers and company. That, of course, had been at night—but many other lives had been lost in the treacherous Channel . . .

Elmore Thompson, a New York City merchant, was soothing his nervous wife. "There'll *be* no more races," he said. "The *Armenia* is too far ahead. We could never catch up to her."

"Well, I hope you're right, Mr. Thompson," she said, fretfully. The baby began to cry and she handed it back to the Negro nursemaid to soothe.

The steam pressure of the *Clay* went up, way up. The ship began to shake and quiver. The furnace doors were kept wide open so the firemen could continually throw shovelfuls of coal onto the red-hot flaming mass inside. As a result, the gusts of burning-hot air that rose to the midship decks made it almost impossible for anyone to pass fore and aft.

Andrew Jackson Dowling, the leading architect of the day, was traveling with his wife and the lovely Widow Wadsworth. He came over to Chief Engineer Johnny Germaine as the latter hung over the rail to cool his lobster-red face. "Chief, is not this racing both imprudent and dangerous?"

"Surely you are not afraid, sir?"

"The ladies are very much afraid."

Chief Germaine smiled indulgently, stroked his sweaty beard. "Ah, the ladies . . . Well, sir, you may tell the ladies—in my name, sir: in my name—that I value the lives of my officers and men. Quite highly, sir. Quite highly." He broke off to greet a gambler. "Hello, Hotaling. How's business?"

Hotaling's teeth showed white as his sun-tanned face broke into a smile. "Kind of slow, Johnny—offering two-to-one on your ship, but everyone's too timid to take it. Afraid the *Armenia*—?"

"Oh, sink and damn the *Armenia!*" roared Germaine. "Two-to-one's not decent odds!"

Bill Hotaling shrugged, gestured. "The *Armenia's* still a mile ahead."

Germaine looked at his rival in the clear summer sunlight, growled. "I'll fix *that*," and went below. In a few minutes the *Henry Clay* began to close in on the other ship. A half-mile . . . a quarter-mile . . . 100 lengths . . . 50 . . . The *Armenia* pulled into Catskill landing only three lengths ahead.

According to Carl Carmer, an authority on Hudson River history, the bow of the *Henry Clay* "cut across the *Armenia's* bow just aft of the larboard wheelhouse." Screams and curses and shouts of alarm rose from both vessels as they crashed.

Quick-witted Dildo Stone shouted, "All passengers to the left side of the ship!" and his officers took up the cry. Those of the 300-odd who were on their feet obeyed, and rushed to the side away from the crash. As a result of this shift of weight, the *Clay's* starboard guard was lifted over and above the larboard (port) guard of the *Armenia*. It stayed there. The *Clay* now had her rival fixed and at her mercy, and Pilot Jim Elmendorf began to drive her toward the west bank of the river.

A scene of terror ensued on the *Armenia*. People knelt to pray, prepared to leap overboard, offered their wallets to the relentless crew of the *Clay*. Some tried to leap from one ship to the other, but were driven back.

"Throw off your steam!" Elmendorf shouted to Polhemius, but the other pilot gritted his teeth and toiled at his wheel, trying in vain to break the grip of the *Clay's* bow.

"Throw off your steam!" Without steam the *Armenia* would be out of the race for good. Polhemius shook his head. The west bank loomed nearer and nearer. Two minutes passed. Three —the screaming from the *Armenia's* women grew louder, was joined by the hoarse cries of the men. Four minutes—

"You'll kill us all, damn your lights and liver!" Polhemius cried. He could count the trees ashore by now. *And* the rocks. "Have mercy!" he shouted, his voice cracking.

Elmendorf's only reply was, "Throw off your steam!"

If Ik Polhemius complied, he and his proud ship would be disgraced forever. But—and here he cast an agonized look at the looming shore—if he didn't—!

Five minutes—Ik sagged. His knees buckled, sweat poured down his seamed face in rivulets. With a trembling hand he gave the signal. The wounded vessel, her pipes giving off a noise like a scream of agony, threw off her steam, and stopped her engines.

A bedlam of cheers arose from the *Henry Clay*—from the ship's company because the race had been won, from the passengers because the race was over. She backed off, releasing the crippled *Armenia*, which drifted listlessly astern. She gave one long whistle in derision—and then steamed down the channel at top speed.

Without a single vessel to race against, the victorious *Henry Clay* was now racing against the record. "We'll set a new one that'll never be beat till the end of all time!" exulted Dildo Stone.

The *Clay* cleared Kingston quickly and tore down the river to Poughkeepsie, lower down on the east bank. Here 20 furious passengers for New York decided to leave the vessel, shouting threats of lawsuits. By the time the *Clay* left Newburgh, her last landing before New York City, the *Armenia* was almost out of sight upriver.

It was hot. The *Clay* continued her dash down mid-channel, passing through the Tappan Zee, widest spot on the River. To the left lay peaceful Sing Sing Village, later renamed "Ossining." Quickly the Palisades loomed up on the right. Shortly before three, as dinner was finishing, the *Henry Clay* passed the Village of Yonkers. A strong wind sprang up, and the ebb tide was flowing against it. There were whitecaps.

About 3:15 the *Armenia*, sulkily beating her way downriver, passed Tarrytown. Ik Polhemius didn't even look ashore at his home town. He felt too ashamed. He took a long look downstream—then another. His astonished yell brought the assistant pilot to his side.

"The *Henry Clay* is nowheres in sight!" Ik said.

"Mebbe she's made Jay Street Docks by now," his aid suggested.

"She can't have!" A sudden thought occurred to him. "Thunderation—she's blowed up and sank!" he cried.

"Precious Lord!" moaned the co-pilot. "Now we never git another chance to beat her!" In a few minutes' time they learned they were both right and wrong.

Shortly before 3 there was another flurry of alarm aboard the *Henry Clay*. A passenger named Henry Lawrence became frightened at a shower of red-hot embers from the smokepipes. He began to drag his baggage forward, erected it into a barricade, and crouched behind it. "Them boilers will blow up, I tell ye!" he yelled. "They'll *explode*!" But everyone laughed at him.

One who didn't laugh was a fireman named Kelly. He was too busy tossing buckets of water on the canvas cover of the larboard boiler. The heat of the metal had caused the cover to burst into flames, and in another minute his shirt had caught fire. Coughing, beating helplessly at the burning garment and trying to tear it from his body, Kelly staggered on deck and—before anyone had a chance to come to his aid—jumped overboard.

Chief Engineer John Germaine sent word to First Mate Stone that the woodwork near boilers and flue had caught fire. And with that, the entire midship section, dried by the day-long furnace heat to the consistency of tinder, burst into flame. No one had to pass the word after that. The ship's plight was obvious.

Pilot Jim Elmendorf saw the spurt of flame as quick as anyone did. He said, in an amazed, almost stunned, tone, "Good Lord, Maggie, the ship's afire!"

Mrs. Elmendorf looked up from her knitting. Very calmly, she said, "Then you had better put her ashore, Mr. Elmendorf"—and went on with her stitches. He saw that no time was to be lost. Signaling for top speed, he spun the wheel. The Hudson at that point, opposite Riverdale, is about two miles wide, and the *Clay* was only a half-mile from the western bank. But for reasons known only to himself and the angels, the *Henry Clay's* pilot headed his vessel for the *eastern* bank—a mile and a half away!

Her brasswork glittering in the mid-afternoon sun, the blazing ship dashed at full speed toward the opposite shore. Clouds of seagulls rose screaming from the river. Assistant Engineer Jacob Zimmerman set her valves for top steam and fixed them. Then he leaped for the deck. The black gang had downed shovels and preceded him, after slamming the furnace doors shut.

The screaming, terrified passengers started to rush forward, but were stopped by a bartender with his own peculiar ideas about safety precautions. "Back!" he shouted. "Get back! The stern will be the safest when we hit!" Most of them obeyed, lined the aft rails shouting for help. In a few minutes time the flames had spread amidships from larboard to starboard so that it was now impossible to go forward at all.

Directly in the path of the doomed ship was the Riverdale estate of Assemblyman Russel Smith, whose gardener was chopping wood on the front terrace. His cry of horrified alarm brought everyone running. The scene, as Smith later described it in a letter, was this: "Down the stream with fearful rapidity came what seemed to be a mass of living fire! It was the steamer *Henry Clay*. Beneath her rolled the waters of the Hudson; above and around her, forked flames darted forth, while at the same moment 100 human voices rent the air with their shrieks!"

All day long the slim white steamer had raced the river. First she had raced against the sister-ship *Armenia*. Then she had raced against time and her own record. Now she was into her last length: she raced against Death itself. And with no one at her furnaces she now made the greatest speed of all, at least 20 knots—almost incredible for a steamer of her capacity and era!

At 3:15, cut athwart by roaring flames, the *Clay* struck the shore with tremendous force, landing at right angles, and plunged up upon the dry land for 25 feet; cutting into and onto a railroad embankment eight feet high. The engines worked perfectly until the last moment. Collyer had built them well . . .

The smokestacks fell crashing to the decks, pinning screaming men and women beneath them. At the moment of collision the furnace doors burst open and spilled their contents of flaming coal upon the stokehold deck. The fire spread at once with terrible speed.

The frightened passenger, Henry Lawrence, was flung to the sandy shore with all his barricade of baggage. He wasn't even bruised. Also thrown to safety by the crash were the pilot, Jim Elmendorf, and his wife, and perhaps 20 or 30 others. About the same number now jumped safely from the bow onto the sand or into the shallow waters. And only now was the terrible result of the bartender's advice apparent. Most of the passengers had stayed aft—the fires prevented their now going forward— and the stern of the ship, where over 200 panic-stricken people milled about in terror, was over deep water!

The wind now began to drive the fires slowly back toward the mass of people. One by one the individual blazes were united into one huge, almost solid, mass of flame. Gradually, relentlessly, it moved aft. Several men began to tug at a big wooden sign advertising "Madame Hortense, Millinery." It resisted them for a moment. Blood spurted from their fingertips. Suddenly it tore loose, and they fell back. The sign clattered to the deck—and at that moment another man darted forward, seized the sign, and leapt overboard with it.

For a single moment he floated safe. Then the huge larboard paddle wheel, beating the water in the ship's death agony, seemed to suck him to it in an instant. While his arms and legs flailed helplessly, and even as his scream still resounded, his head was wedged between wheel and braces. Each huge wooden "bucket," as it came past, beat against his skull until bones, brains, and blood were pounded into a gray-red mass. Then, bereft of steam, the wheels rolled ponderously to a stop.

A. J. Dowling, who could not swim, went systematically about saving lives. Loudly but calmly calling out, "There is no need for panic, ladies—gentlemen," he threw the ship's chairs over the side, helped others to jump. Some caught the chairs and floated to shore, others missed them by inches, went down screaming, fingers clutching futilely.

And all the while, the flames roared . . .

Dowling tossed over the last two chairs. Then, perhaps revealing some long pent-up, Victorian passion, he shoved his wife overboard—seized the Widow Wadsworth in his arms, and leapt into the water.

Thomas Collyer, the *Clay's* owner, reached shore safely. He and others tore apart the palings of the wooden fence there, threw them far out into the river. Many were saved by these, but others drifted against the sides of the burning boat and were drowned in their struggles to get free. Elmore Thompson carefully dragged a settee to the rail and heaved it over. Rather than jump, he began to clamber down. The settee bobbed up beneath him, but at that moment someone struggling in the water grabbed him by the leg. Holding on tightly with both hands, Thompson kicked himself free, but fell into the water. Coming up he looked for the settee, looked for his wife, saw neither. He grabbed hold of a brace. At that moment he saw his wife. Forced from the brace by fire, they both took hold of the wheel itself. Flaming embers rained down upon them, but there was nowhere else to go. And then, as his wife screamed, Thompson felt the wheel turn under their weight...

Scorched by fire, half-drowned, stripped half-naked, the fortunate victims staggered ashore. The less fortunate were still in the water—or on the ship. One man shouted to a terrified young woman, "You cannot hope to make it ashore unless you remove your outer garments—Come: I will jump with you."

Terror gave way before prudery. "I would rather die!" she said. And die she did.

The fire now rushed to devour the rest of the vessel, and most of those aboard prepared to jump. The Hudson River Railroad's southbound train came chugging around the bend from Yonkers just then, and screeched to a halt. Never before had its engineer been stopped by a steamboat across his tracks! Many of the men passengers swam out to the scene of horror.

As the fire ate away at the last standing place, old Stephan Allen took his wife's hand. They leaped together. For a moment his long white hair floated on the surface, then vanished. Mrs. Samuel Cooke, her husband, daughter, and grandson, faced each other. Methodically, Cooke took off his coat, tied his suspenders around his waist, stripped off his shirt. His wife said, "Save yourself, Sam. You can't save all of us and we'll all die if you try to. Water is safer than fire." And before he could stop her, she jumped. Coming to the surface, she realized that enough air was trapped under her hoopskirts to buoy her up for a few minutes—if she didn't struggle.

While the waters boiled with the struggles and screams of others, she calmly floated by with folded hands, until she felt the bottom underfoot.

A Mr. Lauterback of Newark, New Jersey, meanwhile, had saved, one by one, the lives of his nine children. He collapsed after bringing his wife ashore, and was taken to town, unconscious, aboard the train.

Some help had been expected from a broad-beamed sloop nearby. The sloop did put a boat into the water, but the coachman and gardener of Russel Smith got a good look at the men in the boat and realized that "they were two fiends in the shape of men, who did no work of rescue, but plundered the dead." Dashing into the water, the two landsmen got aboard the rowboat and, after a furious struggle, threw the ghouls over the side. One of them kept his hand on the gunwales and attempted to clamber back. The gardener, without a second's pause, pulled his hatchet out of his belt and struck. With a scream of agony the man fell back into the water.

Captain Jack Tallman and his wife somehow got to shore, but there he left her to plunge back into the water. Pale, gaunt, speechless, he toiled like a demon to save the lives his incapacity had imperiled . . . In 20 minutes time it was all over. The *Armenia*, riding the ebb tide at full speed, arrived too late to save any of the living. She picked up many bodies, including that of old Stephan Allen, whose pocket-watch had stopped at 3:26.

By half-past four most of the *Henry Clay* had burned, except a fragment of the bow about 12 feet off the water. This burned slowly, and seemed like some beacon warning off other ships from the mass of charred timber and twisted iron.

Shortly after five the southbound train brought the news to New York City. At first it was believed to be a hoax—there had been one the year before, concerning the steamboat *Reindeer*. But as confirmation arrived, the city was thrown into shock. Many rushed to the scene on the northbound trains, to try to locate relatives and friends. Many arrived in time to identify the dead. Riverdale, now part of the city, at that time was part of Westchester County. As soon as William H. Lawrence, the County Coroner, reached the scene, he impressed local citizens into a coroner's jury and began taking evidence.

Newspaper reporters began their own investigation. "The running ashore was badly done," said the New York *Herald*, the following day. "The bank was sandy, and if the pilot had run the ill-fated ship ashore diagonally (instead of at right angles), many lives could have been saved. The wind was blowing offshore and would have kept the flames at the most advantageous position."

By 9:30 p.m. over 50 bodies had been found, and before the ghastly toll was completed, over 50 more were to turn up. Both Allens were dead. Miss Maria Hawthorne, her uncle, Joseph Dike, Dr. Joe Speed, the "Girl In Bloomer Costume (name unknown),"— the list seemed to go on indefinitely. A Mr. George K. Marker of New York was dragged ashore, drowned.

"I can't understand that," a friend of the dead man said. "George was a powerful good swimmer."

The coroner pointed, wordlessly, to the dead man's money belt. Heavy with gold, it had dragged him to his death at the bottom.

Both Thompsons were saved, but their baby daughter was missing. Late at night, as the death watch torches flared, she was found, clutched in the arms of the Negro maid. All along the river for miles in either direction the torches bobbed. Coroner Lawrence had pitched a tent, and wrote: "The night was remarkably clear, the full moon dimly lighting up the River and the hills . . . The wreck at the bow still burned slowly, revealing in its lurid light the rows of corpses, and the people trying to identify them. The surface of the stream, placid and silent as the grave itself, was broken only by the oars of those still dredging for bodies . . ."

At midnight the alarm was given, echoing from mid-channel: "*Ghouls! Ghouls! Corpse-robbers!*"

"A dark craft filled with plunderers," wrote the coroner, "filled with sacrilegious harpies, was hovering about." The coroner and his jurymen were armed, and they fired into the dim, moonlit night. A cry of pain, quickly cut off, came out of the darkness. The "dark craft" vanished.

Next morning, among the bodies recovered was that of architect Dowling. The arms of the beautiful Widow Wadsworth were still clasped tightly around him. All day long and all the following night the cannons boomed, their vibrations bringing up the dead. The bodies, covered with green boughs in lieu of sheets, lay dotting the banks for miles.

Altogether, there were over 100 dead—most of them from drowning, few from burns.

Bill Hotaling, the riverboat gambler, who had saved dozens of lives—but had failed to rescue the poor "Bloomer Girl"—drank himself into a stupor.

It was reported that President Millard Fillmore wept when he read the reports.

In New York City some wept, but others were moved to rage. Public meetings denounced the owners and crews of both the *Henry Clay* and *Armenia*. The owners promptly publicized their no-racing compact. "What was it, then, if not a race?" demanded the *Herald's* James Gordon Bennett. "It was an unfortunate accident," said Thomas Collyer.

Westchester County arrested Collyer, Germaine, Tallman, Elmendorf, and Stone; charged them on the odd-sounding count of "criminal murder." But County Judge Edmondson reduced the charges to manslaughter and released them on bail. In September the steamboat *Reindeer,* racing against the *Rochester*, blew her starboard boiler. Bennett, Horace Greeley of the *Tribune*, Raymond of the *Times*, and other newspaper publishers demanded an end to racing.

The trial was an anticlimax. The prosecution failed to prove criminal intent, and all the defendants were acquitted on November 2nd. But one good thing did result from the agitation: Congress, stung into action, passed the Steamboat Inspection Act, ending forever the thrilling but deadly sport of racing engine-propelled ships on the Hudson River. The 100 victims of the *Henry Clay* had not died in vain.

BEER LIKE WATER

A HUGE GREAT-GRANDDADY OF A RAT leaped out of the tangled mass of rubbish which packed the lower part of the conduit and jumped at one of the men. The man screamed, tried to flee, his rubber boots slipping on the slimy surface beneath his feet. For a second, panic threatened. Then there was a sharp report which echoed and re-echoed, the rat fell writhing in the filthy muck and was immediately stomped to death by the man who had shot it.

Joe Horvath waved his revolver in one hand and his lamp in the other. "Come on," he said, impatiently. "Let's go—what're you waiting for?"

The answer—as the frightened Department of Public Works crew huddled fearfully together—came from the shadows surrounding them. As the last echoes of the shot died away, a chorus of squeaks and scrabbling sounds came from the darkness. Just outside of the beam of lamplight, grey forms darted, red eyes gleamed. "What makes them damn rats grow so big?" someone muttered.

"There must be millions of them!" another protested. "They bite you—you could get hydrophobia!"

"You'll got worse than that from me!" Joe Horvath threatened. "Let's *go!*" He shone his light around, muttered disgustedly. "Look at all this junk—bedsprings, old mattresses, auto seats, Christmas trees, boxes, crates. No wonder the creek backs up— no wonder it smells bad. We got to get this crap out of here." He gestured to the men. They moved forward slowly—but they moved. You didn't argue with Joe Horvath. And above all, even when he had no revolver, you didn't call him any dirty names. Because if you did he would hit you ten or twenty times, and if you fell down, he would pick you up so he could hit you ten or twenty times more and knock you down again. Joe had a temper.

He moved along, holding his revolver on the ready. He gnawed his cigar and muttered into his mustache. His being down here in the filthy, cluttered conduit through which the Nepperhan Creek ran into the Hudson was in the nature of a punishment detail. Everyone knew that. He couldn't be fired for telling the big-shots what he really thought of them. Horvath was a war veteran and he did his work well. But he *could* be given the dirty work to do—and he was. Like now.

Yonkers politics smelled about as sweet as the Nepperhan itself—and the lower part of it formed part of the sewage system. Lately, the merchants whose back premises faced the last open section of the Creek (or River, as it was also called)—a block formed by Warburton Avenue, Main Street, North Broadway, and Manor Hall Square—had been complaining that the Nepperhan smelled worse than usual. So that was why the D.P.W. crew was down here in the muck. The day was September 29, the year was 1930—and a man was lucky to have any job at all. There was a Depression going on. The three main industries of Yonkers (the Otis Elevator Company, the Alexander Smith Carpet Factory, and the Spreckels Sugar Refinery) were all hard hit.

Only the bootleggers were doing well. Repeal of Prohibition was still three years in the future. But not everyone had the good luck to work for a bootlegger.

Joe Horvath's voice exploded in a shout of disgust. "Who the Hell threw this into the Creek? And what the Hell is it, anyway?" *This* looked like it was a pipe or hose of some kind. It was about four inches in diameter and was bound tightly around with wire. "Copper wire," Joe observed, thoughtfully. "*Nobody* would throw away this much copper wire . . . Where does it come from?" He shone the light backwards, then forwards. But the hose seemed to have neither beginning nor end. "That's a funny thing," he muttered. "A damn funny thing."

One of the men suggested, diffidently, "Maybe you look in chart, Joe—dem maps you got from City Hall. Maybe is *supposed* to be pipe here, huh?"

Joe shook his head. "I know what's on the charts," he said. "And there's no pipe supposed to be here. And no hose, neither . . . I never *saw* a hose like this. All right." Abruptly, he made up his mind. "Let's all grab ahold and when I give the signal, we pull." The men laid aside their tools, wiped their hands, seized the funny-looking pipe—or hose, or whatever it was. "All ready? Get set. *Pull!*"

The men gave a tremendous tug. The hose went taut. They jerked once more. Then it gave way, the men went tumbling and sliding backwards. Somewhere off in the darkness the heard a splash—a sound of something gushing. "We broke it for sure," someone said. Then he sniffed. A heavy bittersweet smell met their noses, drowning out the stale odor of the conduit. Joe lifted his head, took a deep breath, let it out.

"That can't be what I think it is—can it?" he asked, incredulous.

But one of the D.P.W. men was less skeptical. He took a step forward, his boots squilching. "Maybe it can't be—but it is! It's beer!" he yelled. "It's *beer!*"

For a long time the City of Yonkers had wanted to cover over the whole of the Nepperhan where it ran through the central part of town—a trickle in dry weather, a torrent in wet. But they were stymied by a strip of land sixteen feet long and eight feet wide on either side of the Creek a block from the Getty Square area. It was known as No Man's Land because it wasn't carried on the tax rolls and no one knew who owned it. Maybe it still belonged to the Indians. So the only answer to the smells and the stenches which rose from the open part of the Creek bed was to send a crew of men to clean the stream out whenever it got too raunchy.

Near an open manhole another, smaller D.P.W. crew was standing by with a truck on which a sewer-cleaning apparatus was fixed. They talked idly together while they waited on word from Joe Horvath to start dipping up the debris, but their talk didn't deal with the ownership of No Man's Land. There were two big topics of conversation—the Depression—Repeal. Governor Franklin D. Roosevelt had suggested opening all National Guard Armories in New York State to house jobless, homeless men in the forthcoming winter. Both he and Tuttle, the Republican candidate for governor, favored repeal. So did Al Smith.

Suddenly there was a burst of noise from the manhole. "Whatsa matta?" one of the D.P.W. men asked. The noise grew nearer, louder.

"Somebuddy git hoit?" his partner inquired.

They gathered around the opening in the street. As they watched a face appeared. It was excited and disheveled, but it was definitely not worried. "*Beer*!" the face yelled. "*Beer*! *Beer*! *Beer*!" Passers-by stopped, came over to watch what was going on. Why were all the men climbing up from the manhole? Why were they dancing and capering? True, it was a lovely, crisp, late September day, but—

"Ah, whatta ya givin' me?" scoffed one of the men at the D.P.W. truck. "What beer? Where beer?" A sudden thought occurred to him. "Y'mean they found some bottles—or barrels—of beer down there?"

The sewer cleaners hauled away at something—a pipe—or a hose—pulled it to the surface. A steady gush of some amber-colored liquid came from the loose end. One of them bent over and drank. Another one exclaimed, happily, "No bottles—no barrels —just like it comes—*beer*!" Someone protested that it was impossible, someone else that it was unsanitary. "Whaddaya mean, 'unsanitary'?" the man who was drinking paused to protest. "Beer's got alcohol in it, ain't it? So the alcohol inna beer disinfecks it!"

This bit of scientific information instantly convinced the skeptic. He looked for a cup or a glass, and, finding none, stuffed his sandwiches in his pocket and filled the lower part of his lunch-box with the foaming brew. The knot of spectators swelled to a group, then to a crowd. The happy word was passed from person to person, from house to house. It was carried by men passing by in cars, and by people who rushed to the telephone. Thoughtful children informed their parents.

The cry went up all along Park Hill Avenue and School Street, where the discovery was made—"*Beer! Beer! It's running in the street! Free beer!*"—through New Main Street into Getty Square, the heart of downtown Yonkers, up North Broadway, down South Broadway—"*Beer! Beer! Beer!*"

"Come and get it! Free beer!" The citizens heard, they came, and they got it. They came with cups and glasses, bottles and buckets, jugs, jars, pots, pans, pails, basins, cans, tins, tankards —anything that would hold liquid. They were very, very happy. And then, just when the singing and dancing had about commenced, the steady flow began to slacken, died down to a trickle, stopped dead. A great groan of disappointment went up.

The beer, to be sure, had had a faint taste of rubber to it. But after 11 years of Prohibition, everyone was used to beer tasting strongly of much worse things than rubber. Anybody in Yonkers in 1930 who objected to a mild flavor of latex in his brew was liable to stand accused of being a Communist, or—what was much worse—an Englishman.

So no one complained about the beer's taste—only that there was no more of it. The crowd stood around waiting hopefully, until, finally, the police arrived and began to move them on.

Joe Horvath, meanwhile, had preceded his men out of the conduit, and immediately notified his superior, Deputy Public Works Commissioner Kearns. "And that," said an old timer recently, discussing the case; "That was where Kearns lost his head. That was where Kearns cut his own throat. Instead of hushing it up right away, Kearns *told*."

One of the people Kearns told was the mayor.

The mayor of Yonkers at that time was a Republican (the Democrats had lost out in the preceding election), the Honorable John J. Fogarty. As a former FBI man and former United States

Attorney as well, he was familiar with the ins and outs of Prohibition Law enforcement—and non-enforcement.

Fogarty listened as Kearns blurted out the story. He was young, capable, personable, intelligent, and handsome. *Everyone* loved Jack Fogarty, and agreed that he was on the threshold of a great career. Unfortunately, he never got to cross the threshold. He suffered from a singular delusion. It was His Honor's profound conviction that, if he only tried hard enough, he could drink up all the liquor in Westchester County all by himself. He died broke but game, still trying.

If the thought of all that good beer running through the gutters of his fair city disturbed the mayor, he didn't say so. Instead, he asked Kearns, "Who else knows?"

"Well," said the D.P.W. official, "Iron Mike knows. I told him."

Fogarty nodded at this mention of Police Chief E. J. Quirk's nickname. "Who else?"

Kearns hesitated, then blurted out the truth. "Half the people in Yonkers, by now, I guess . . . We'll have to notify the Feds, won't we?"

The mayor said, "I guess we will." He didn't sound at all happy.

And so the City of Yonkers (later on it called itself "The City of Gracious Living" in an expensive publicity campaign which fooled nobody) made headlines all over the nation. Yonkers is reached—assuming that anyone *wants* to reach it—by heading north through the west Bronx. At that time it had a bit over a hundred thousand people and wasn't too sure if it was an industrial city or a residential suburb of New York. It still isn't sure.

In the Fall of 1930, despite Prohibition and despite Depression, many Yonkers merchants were doing a brisk trade in all the equipment needed for the Do-It-Yourself School of moonshining: canned malt and hop syrups, bottles, cappers, crockery, grape juice, charred kegs, and copper devices which a little effort could convert into efficient stills. But the police weren't interested in wiping out the nefarious tools of home brew, nor was the Bureau of Prohibition. It was too universal, too hard to get convictions.

Beer pipes leading through (or under) the city streets, however, were not at all. Not one bit.

The Yonkers *Herald* for September 30, 1930, gave its headline to Governor Roosevelt's re-nomination by acclamation. New York City police, the paper said on page one, were still looking for Justice Crater who had vanished two months earlier (theoretically, they are still looking—at least, they haven't found him yet). And inside, on page two, on the bottom, was a tiny paragraph entitled POLICE ARE PROBING SEWER LIQUOR HOSE.

The Department of Justice men, led by a Captain O'Connel, arrived on the scene. Chief Quirk and his men were already there. Another squad of D.P.W. men was sent underground, with strict instructions not to sample the merchandise, but to trace the hose. It led to a garage at the junction of School and Herriot Streets. Herriot was a poor but respectable thoroughfare. School Street was merely poor, the subject of a thousand dirty jokes.

This time, however, the professional ladies looked out their windows with unworried interest at the forces of the law. A large crowd of people gathered to watch. The garage had a door of reinforced steel. It was locked. No one, apparently, was at home.

"We'll soon have it open," one of the Prohibs said, confidently, limbering up his acetylene torch and going to work. All he really had to do, of course, was to cut out the lock. But the crowd's presence appealed to his sense of the dramatic. While they watched admiringly, the Federal agent proceeded to cut an opening large enough for a fat man in a silk hat to pass through. As the panel fell away Captain O'Connel and Police Chief Quirk made their way inside.

And at once reappeared, rather purple around the chops.

"There's another damned door there, with *more* steel plating!" the Chief said.

"Bring that torch in and open it," Captain O'Connel ordered his man. The latter hung back, bashfully.

"I can't, Captain," he said, squirming. "I haven't got no more fuel!"

The crowd waited patiently till another tank of fuel was brought and the second portal was broached. Then, moving as cautiously as if they expected to find the Hunkpapa Sioux barricaded in the grease-pits, the police and Federal agents moved in with revolvers drawn.

But the place was empty. Bottle-caps were scattered on the floor. A genial odor of malt and hops permeated the garage. In one corner of the concrete floor a trench was gouged out—it led to a hole. Someone idly kicked a bottle-cap into the opening. There was a moment's wait, then a tiny splash.

"What's your opinion of all this, Chief?" Captain O'Connel asked. (A rumor, meanwhile, spread through the crowd outside that Judge Crater's body had been found inside. The popular consensus was that they would rather have beer.)

"I'll tell you what my opinion is," Iron Mike said, portentously. "My opinion is, that this place has been equipped and used as a beer-bottling plant." Captain O'Connel nodded his head slowly at this sage deduction, and said he didn't wonder but what the Chief might well be right. "It's my further opinion," Quirk continued, "that the operator of this bottling plant became aware of the police surveillance, and removed the equipment."

Just how the equipment had been removed without the police surveillance being at all aware of it was not explained.

"In that case," suggested the Federal officer, "the pipe or hose may have led here from a brewery." Iron Mike said he wouldn't be a bit surprised. After some more of the Sherlock Holmes bit, the two men decided it might be a good idea to trace the hose the other way, and see where it led in the opposite direction. But, as it was getting late, they decided to do this tomorrow. The Department of Justice men went back to New York, and the local police returned to their headquarters on Wells Avenue.

Some of the crowd, disappointed at the lack of action, went home. Some, guided by the peculiar psychology of crowds, stayed on to gape at the empty garage. And some, there being no television in those days, decided to pay social calls at several School Street establishments which were known always to welcome company. It was the best night the ladies had had since the bottom fell out of Wall Street the year before.

The D.P.W. men, meanwhile, had been hauling fathoms and fathoms of hose up out of the sewers. Kearns approached his superior, Commissioner William Colquohon. "Ah—what'll I do with the hose, Bill?" he inquired.

Colquohon glared at him. "What the hell are you asking *me* for?" he growled. "You went to the mayor first, didn't you? Then ask the mayor what to do with the hose!" And with a graphic but impracticable suggestion of what else the unhappy Kearns might do with the hose, the annoyed Commissioner stomped away. If Deputy Commissioner Kearns had the idea that his political career had met up with a check, he was absolutely right.

The hose was cut into manageable lengths and stored in the Police garage.

At four o'clock in the morning a man was found by the police fiddling with the cover of a manhole at the corner of New Main and Brooks Streets, a few blocks from the garage. He gave a New York City address and said that he was a truck-driver's assistant and had come back to look for a missing package.

"You expect to find it in the sewer?" a policeman asked him.

"I come along and I see the, now, manhole cover is off," the man said. "So I put it back. See? Any, now, citizen would of done the same," he added, virtuously. The man was questioned and released. The address he gave proved to be a false one.

And in the morning, when the forces of the law turned up to trace the other part of the hose—surprise, surprise—it had disappeared. The police professed themselves utterly mystified.

A life-long resident of the City of Gracious Living, now a lawyer with the Federal government, observed recently: "At that time the population of Yonkers was equally divided between bootleggers and those under eighteen years of age." But other worthy citizens deny that this is strictly accurate—quite a number of Yonkers bootleggers, they point out, were themselves under eighteen years of age. However this may be, while every city in the United States had beer barons and rumrunners, it does seem that Yonkers had more than its share.

There were several reasons for this. The city was located on the lower Hudson River, a large body of easily navigable water. It contained, on Ann Street, a "permit brewery"—one which was licensed to make "near" or "de-alcoholized" beer—and so was able to procure (and to dispose of) practically unlimited quantities of malt, barley, and hops. Right on the Yonkers river front was a huge plant for refining sugar and another one for distilling grain alcohol (only for "industrial" purposes, of course)—both being essential commodities for the moonshine business.

The City of Yonkers was also located right next to the six or seven million perpetually thirsty inhabitants of the City of New York—a great bottomless gullet of a market.

And in addition, it was for a time at least the residence of an entrepreneur named Arthur Flegenheimer. Also known as The Dutchman. Also known as Dutch Schultz, "the King-Pin of New York bootlegging."

Apparently the rocks and rills, the woods and templed hills, of upper Palisade Avenue appealed to The Dutchman's taste. And besides, if he leaned far enough out of his garden, and if the wind was in the right direction, he could have spit practically onto the roof of the Ann Street brewery. Not that he would have done such a thing, because he owned the biggest piece of it. He was joined in this business venture by a few fellow-gangsters such as Owney Madden—and (so it was rumored) several prominent Westchester citizens of good reputation.

The piece of land where the malt-house was located was known as Chicken Island. School Street was its main thoroughfare—there weren't many others. If the legal authorities suspected that the pipeline led from a brewery in Yonkers (and not, say, one in Texas), their puzzlement as to where the brewery was located is hard to understand. There was only the one in the whole city, and its presence was perfectly legal. It had a permit from the Treasury Department to make "near" beer.

This being so, it is also hard to understand why passers-by were so unhospitably discouraged. A Yonkers barber complained only recently, with indignation still green after thirty-two years, that even the most pressing kidney condition was not accepted as excuse for pausing in Ann Street after dark. A Yonkers merchant recalls that in those days he was once stopped in Ann Street by a man on horseback.

"It wasn't exactly a horse," he says; "more like an Indian pony. And this fellow says to me, 'Where do ya think you're going?' I say, 'Through here and into Palisade Avenue.' 'Ah, no, you're not—turn around and go back.' And he pulls out a gun when I try to argue with him. I says, 'You're right!'—and I turned around and went back. Oh, sure, I told the police. And they said 'Kid, you been seeing too many movies'!"

There were, indeed, a few suspicious souls who wondered why an expert German braumeister should be hired at a fabulous salary to make "*near*" beer. But with armed and mounted guards protecting the honor of the brewery, nobody was going to risk hurting their feelings by wondering out loud.

Three days after the first finding of the beer hose and its glorious aftermath, the story was again reduced to a tiny paragraph on an inside page.

LACK OF CLUES IN BEER HOSE CASE

Although the garage is still being watched, police have failed to find any clues to the ownership of the beer-bottling plant believed to have been operated there. The section of hose is still being held in Police headquarters.

Maybe the cops were waiting for someone to come and claim it.

Anyway, there were more important pieces of news. An epidemic of infantile paralysis had emptied Wesleyan University, and there was a pre-Salk attempt to treat it with serum. Madame Curie was reported near a new cancer discovery, using radium. There was a very modern note: CHINESE REDS AGAIN FIRE

UPON U.S. CRAFT. And there was an odd story about a six-year-old boy refused admission to school in Ohio because of what the paper delicately termed "his unusual development." The kid had a baritone voice, the strength of a fifteen-year-old boy, smoked cigars, and shaved regularly.

And there was a red-hot scoop: *Officer Stops Runaway Horse.*

For almost two weeks the Yonkers *Herald* happily forgot about the beer-hose scandal, even if nobody else in town did.

On October 14 the Nepperhan Avenue sewer collapsed with a roar. It was the oldest one in the city, and how the politicians and contractors—who tore everything else in Yonkers up every two years—had overlooked it for four decades was a mystery.

The Department of Public Works sent another crew down to repair it—or at least to investigate it—and guess what they found? *Right!*

This time there was no public hooraw. The D.P.W. foreman ordered his men to keep their mouths shut while he went to report this latest liquid bonanza. Not a one of them stuck his head above the surface, but their mouths did not remain altogether—or at least, not entirely—shut. By the time they were ordered out they were thoroughly sozzled. Even the rats were drunk. Sewer work had *never* been so popular!

Down came Iron Mike Quirk, determined to plumb this mystery to the depths. Down came Captain O'Connel, well primed with enough fuel this time to cut his way into the Subtreasury Building vaults.

The hose was traced from Nepperhan Avenue and Elm Street, down Elm to Palisade Avenue, down Palisade to Engine Place (a low-rent neighborhood inhabited chiefly by citizens of Nigerian extraction), and through to John Street. It stopped just short of a John Street garage which bore a large VACANCY—FOR RENT sign. But the peace officers, their suspicions unaccountably aroused, forced their way into the vacant building, and found an elaborate bottling plant and enough beer to drown the whole police force.

"If this keeps on," said O'Connel, "we're going to run out of garages . . . where do you keep the *cars* in Yonkers, anyway, Quirk?"

"Arrest these men," directed the Police Chief, ignoring the witticism. There were nine of the malefactors, and all of them—together with a sample of the beer—were removed to the Federal Court in New York City. The nine men seemed oddly unworried, probably because they had been warned in enough time to run several hundred gallons of the Nepperhan Creek into the vats with the beer.

Sure enough, the Federal analysts reported that the liquor wasn't even strong enough to constitute "near" beer, and the men were released—presumably to go look for more garages.

By this time more than six thousand feet, or more than a mile, of hose had been pulled up from underneath the Yonkers streets. And neither the local police nor the Department of Justice agents had been able to figure out where in the *Hell* it had been carrying beer from. "Probly comes from some 'now' broory," they kept repeating, and never once took a stroll toward the one on Ann Street—the only one in the city—which was several times the size of the elephant house in the Bronx Zoo, with barbed wire on top of its walls, and armed guards mounting pony patrol outside twenty-four hours a day.

Finally, on October 16, the Federal Grand Jury swung into action. They issued subpoenas for the Commissioner and Deputy Commissioners of Public Works, the Chief of Police, the Captain of the 1st Precinct, the Fire Chief and the Deputy Fire Chief. (The implication about the last two was not that they had supplied fire hose to pump beer, but to find out if they'd noticed anything funny while making regular building inspections.)

But before any of the subpoenas were served, Mayor Jack Fogarty had swung into action. He ordered all city officials and employees to appear voluntarily before the Grand Jury if their presence should be desired. Assistant U.S. Attorney Watts said that he wasn't accusing anybody. "I don't even know if any Yonkers officials had even heard about the hose line before it was publicized. All I'd like to know," he said, a trifle desperately, "is just how more than a mile of four-inch hose could be run under Columbus Avenue, Elm Street, Palisade Avenue, and John Street, without any knowledge on the part of city officials or employees."

People in Yonkers thought that was a good question. They would still like to know.

And finally Watts pointed the finger no one else had dared to point. "After more than six thousand feet of hose worth more than $25,000," he said, "had been hauled from various manholes, it was realized that one of these manholes was only about two hundred yards from the brewery of the State Cereal Company at Ann and Edward Streets. After the first pipe line was discovered," Watts went on, "both ends were cut."

Who cut them?

Deputy Public Works Commissioners D. R. Dedrick and James J. Kearns, Police Chief E. J. Quirk, Water Superintendent Oscar D. Barker, Police Captain William H. Crough of the 1st Precinct, Detective Sergeant Henry F. Murphy, and Detective Joseph Sullivan volunteered to appear before the Federal Grand Jury.

Iron Mike Quirk said that Kearns told him that all the sewers in which the hoses were laid "were over four feet in diameter. So it would be possible for men to remove a single manhole cover and thread the hose for as great a distance as they wanted to. Suppose the policeman on beat was somewhere else on his post at the time? Detection would have been impossible."

In other words, if a policeman saw six thousand feet of hose slithering into a manhole, he would suspect nothing unless there was a man attached to it in plain sight.

Meanwhile, a third D.P.W. crew had engaged in what was rapidly becoming Yonkers's favorite outdoor sport. They went out to clean out a clogged drain. They shot some big rats—the secret of the huge size of Yonkers sewer-rats had been solved, even if nothing else had: they had grown fat on mash—and they came across a huge length of mysterious wire-bound rubber hose. But this time, alas, the line was dry, and the Public Works employees were feeling quite savage about it.

Deputy Commissioner Dedrick had a theory about this last line. "It ran downhill," he said; "and I believe it was *floated* down to wherever it was floated down to." As usual, both terminals had been cut.

But U.S. Attorney Watts wasn't buying that theory. "The hose couldn't go around corners and make angles from one street to another without someone opening manholes and going down to guide it. How is it possible," he burst out, querulously, "for all this to have been done without being seen?"

Was everyone in Yonkers blind? Or was everyone in Yonkers in on the secret?

The New York *Daily News* advanced a theory of its own. "A former Yonkers police official" was cited, anonymously, as source. He said the purpose of the hose was not so much to baffle the police as the Treasury Department's "beer-checkers." These were the Federal inspectors supposed to be on duty in the "permit" breweries to see that all beer was de-alcoholized. "This beer-checker was demanding a cut on all the beer that went out without being weakened, and the pipeline was used to get the stuff out without his knowledge. No matter how much it cost to lay the hose, it was worth it in the savings on big graft assessments," said the ex-cop.

Could be.

It turned out that the Yonkers police had never turned in a written report on the discovery of even the first pipeline. Chief Quirk was asked if he would waive immunity. He replied emphatically that he would.

The New York *Mirror* suggested that "the law enforcement officials may have got honest, or—" dismissing this as too unlikely for further consideration—"raised their commission on each barrel necessitating this shrewd expedient. This is the sort of brain-work that keeps us in beer. It deserves public applause."

Dutch Schultz, of course, didn't feel like applauding. But although he would have shot down as many gangsters as got in his way, there was nothing he could do to rub out a Federal Grand

Jury.

Meanwhile—who owned the garages that the pipelines had been traced to? "The authorities," said the Yonkers *Herald*, "are busily engaged in tracing the proprietors . . ."

The hose was examined by experts, who said that it was especially heavy to prevent seepage from the sewers. There was talk that it would be analyzed to determine who had made it, in hopes this would lead to the purchaser. Nothing ever came of this plan.

Traffic, meanwhile, at the Ann Street brewery slackened considerably. Closed moving vans, which had stopped in great numbers at the garage-pumping stations, moved no more. As a result of the temporary drought, it was rumored that humanitarian bootleggers from Jersey would bring in relief convoys. George Salburg, Police Commissioner of Poughkeepsie, was told to watch the Mid-Hudson Bridge and head off these philanthropists.

Nobody said anything about watching the Yonkers Ferry.

Dutch Schultz flew into a mad rage and threatened to shoot his lawyer, "Dixie" Davis, the "Kid Mouthpiece," who had been entrusted with paying off the protection money.

"Arthur," said Dixie, speaking very softly, "that brewery was registered in the name of our 'front,' but the 'front' signed it over to me. I couldn't get any life insurance because I'm in the racket —but if I should die suddenly, Arthur, why, that brewery would belong to *my* family, Arthur . . ."

The Dutchman calmed down at once. He smiled, threw his arm around Dixie's shoulders. "Why, Sonny Boy," he said, "you know that I wouldn't hurt a hair on your head . . ."

Several years later it turned out that both Schultz *and* Davis had been taken for a sleigh ride on the Yonkers deal. They thought they had been paying off Police Chief Quirk, and they hadn't. Not at all. They had been paying off a local politico who had passed himself off as Quirk to the two of them, without Iron Mike's knowing anything about it. Iron Mike, it is said, was very much enraged when he found this out.

The Yonkers *Herald*, meanwhile, still trying to pay as little attention to the sordid details of the beer-pipe scandal, ran a piece on the history of the lute. They traced it to the Arabic "al-ud," and mentioned its connection with the medieval theorbo and cittern, the Biblical psalter and the modern zither.

Professor Carlton of Syracuse, the candidate for governor of the Law Preservation (or Dry) Party, spoke in Yonkers.

Sewers, he said, were the right place for beer. "End 'Repeal' talk!" the prof urged. "Stiffen the anti-liquor laws! No home can be happy and safe where the sting of the liquor serpent is felt, and while the bootlegger is abroad in the land!"

On October 27th, however, the *Herald* had to forget about the zither and the lute, because an all-too-well-founded rumor was abroad in the land that a *fourth* length of pipe had been found in a sewer under Nepperhan Avenue. This was soon after the Grand Jury had begun its look-see; the authorities were fed up to their ear lobes with beer-hose, and since this batch was found neatly coiled up under a garage near Warburton Avenue, they simply removed it without saying a word for publication.

But word got out, of course.

Public Works Commissioner Colquohon was summoned before the Grand Jury. But instead of asking him about underground hose, they asked if he knew anything about beer-runners —i.e. bootleggers who operated on the surface, but who didn't handle the hard stuff. The Commissioner declared with great fervor that he had never heard of such a thing. So far as he knew, no one in the City of Yonkers drank anything stronger than Orange Crush or Moxie.

And then the Nepperhan Avenue sewer collapsed *again*! By this time Colquohon was afraid to go look. He didn't even like to use a rubber hose to water his lawn. The bootleggers should remove their own damned pipelines. Why the hell should the Department of Public Works do it for them?

The next day the *Herald* had three interesting bits of news on the same page—an inside page. Chiang Kai-shek was baptized. Louis Freitag was charged with hitting Alexander Schwartz on the head with a salami which Schwartz, a delicatessen proprietor, had refused to skin. And the third bit was headed, BEER HOSE PROBE OFF. GRAND JURY TO DEFER LOCAL CASE TO CONSIDER OTHERS.

That, in effect, was that. The probe never really got under way again. It was pointed out that the work of laying the hoses may have been superintended by a hydraulic engineer—that it was bound with wire only at low points, to withstand high pressures. The Grand Jury paid no attention. It was hinted that maybe it was not a hydraulic engineer after all, but someone in an allied profession—someone in fairly high office in the City of Gracious Living. The Grand Jury said to go away and not bother it.

Ten years later the *Herald*, its identity now merged with its former competitor, the *Statesman*, summed the matter up like this: "Authorities evidently decided they just couldn't put their fingers on the man or men who were responsible for the remarkably clever job of installing 6,000 feet of thick hose in a city sewer without anyone catching on."

But a lot had happened in the intervening decade. For example, in 1932 Terry Brady blew the whistle on Dutch Schultz. Terry operated a small weekly of the "personal journalism" variety, running fierce front-page editorials denouncing everyone and everything—animal, vegetable, or mineral—which he signed "Captain Terence A. Brady." A veteran of the A.E.F., he was the only ex-serviceman in Yonkers who continued to use his old title (except for Admiral Harrington, who had been a midshipman in the Civil War).

In April, 1932, the Captain decided that he didn't like Dutch Schultz. Every hood on the east coast was scared witless of the Dutchman, but this didn't faze Terry Brady. He came out with an extra exposing Schultz's connection with the Chicken Island brewery, and demanding to know why the authorities didn't Do Something About It.

The Dutchman heard about it, and as fast as the bundles of Yonkers *Records* were dumped off at the newsstands, a black Cadillac full of goons picked them up, paid the dealers a dollar for each copy, and zoomed off for the next drop. As soon as they had gone away, the Captain happily ran off an extra extra and rushed it to the stands.

The authorities didn't do a damned thing. It was hinted that Schultz's difficulties with Brady were due to his having grown tired of paying blackmail. But the Captain said that this was a vile canard spread by his political enemies—of which, heaven knows, he had more than enough to satisfy a hundred other men.

In March of 1938, Mrs. Florence Flegenheimer, widow of Dutch Schultz, shook the City of Yonkers by suing one Thomas A. Brogan for $109,264 worth of stock in the Chicken Island brewery. She also sued Dixie Davis, who had troubles of his own, having been put in jail by N. Y. District Attorney (later Governor) Dewey.

Mrs. F.'s claim was, that in 1930 and again in 1932 her late husband and a few others had organized two dummy corporations to mask his ownership of the brewery, and that the brewery had somehow gotten into the hands of Mr. Brogan. Besides being the president of the malthouse, Mr. Brogan was also a leading paving contractor. He also happened to be State Democratic Committeeman. He was, at least in Yonkers, a Very Big Man.

The gangster's widow charged in her affidavit: "That the defendant Brogan at that time was and still is the Democratic and political boss of the City of Yonkers; that it was necessary to obtain protection in order to operate the brewery during Prohibition without interference from the Yonkers authorities . . . Brogan was the man that had to be seen in that connection . . .

"[It was] advised that $2,500 per week would be required to be paid off by my husband to operate during that period . . . my husband paid over to Brogan personally $2,500 each and every week for protection . . . and it is needless to say that neither [the brewery], its operations, output, and trucks were interfered with nor interrupted by the Yonkers authorities . . ."

Mr. Brogan called the lady's charges "scurrilous." He said he was not the political boss of Yonkers, either. He denied that he ever received "any money or monies for protection or otherwise . . . At no time in his career was he ever associated or connected with the said Arthur Flegenheimer"—i.e., Dutch Schultz.

The brewery went into receivership. Mrs. F. never got a dime.

If anybody, whoever it was, accepted $2,500 a week for protecting the brewery, he made a lousy deal. It has been estimated on damned good authority that the Chicken Island suds shop made a clear profit of $10,000 *a day*! Figure that out over the course of a year. $2,500 a week protection was nothing. $25,000 for wire reinforced hose was nothing. And, after Repeal, and her husband's murder, that's what the Dutchman's widow had left —nothing. She learned stenography and got a job in an office to support herself and her children.

So then, what is the answer after all to the Big Question? How *did* the hose get into the sewers without anyone noticing? The answer is that plenty of people noticed—but they didn't pay any attention. The hose-layers used a truck painted to look exactly like that used by the local phone company. Those who bothered to watch as they passed by simply took it for granted that insulated phone cables were being laid underground.

And the politician who found the biggest lot of hose-pipe and did not report it to the FBI was never even questioned by the FBI and was never even questioned by the Grand Jury. How do I know? He told me so himself.

What happened to all the figures in The Great Beer-Pipe Scandal? Dutch Schultz was shot down by some disgruntled business rivals while on a trip to Newark. Although police stenographers took down all his dying words, no one was ever able to figure out what the weird recital meant. Iron Mike Quirk died of a heart attack while on an auto jaunt with a lady friend. (His successor shot himself on the eve of another investigation.) Joe Horvath (not his real name) went into business, and is still doing well, not taking nothing from nobody.

The Dutchman's "Kid Mouthpiece" Dixie Davis got out of jail, married the sweetheart with whom the kindly police had allowed frequent hotel rendezvous; he went straight and vanished from sight. Captain Terence A. Brady, the wildcat publisher, drew a suspended sentence for publishing "indecent" material in his little paper—it was a bum rap, he said, inspired by his Political Enemies—and expired a few years ago from natural causes. This was a big surprise to Yonkers, which always expected he would sooner or later be shot dead.

As for the gentleman who is said to have collected the protection money under the pretense that he was Chief Quirk, he is still alive and powerful. Anyone in Yonkers will tell you his name. But no one will allow himself to be quoted. Not even now, thirty-two years later.

And that about winds up the story of the Great Beer-Hose Affair. But the memory lingers on. The Beer-Pipe is to Yonkers what the Headless Horseman is to Tarrytown—a beloved legend. Its very recollection is fragrant. Once upon a time (the people of Yonkers like to remember), when the Depression was hard upon the land, someone struck the flinty pavement of their city, and for one wild, sweet hour, it gushed forth with a fountain of pure, free beer.

THE MEN WHO KILLED THE BRIGADE

MINIÉ RIFLES CRACKED in the darkness. The great bell of the Russian Orthodox Cathedral in besieged Sebastopol tolled midnight. The deep notes were heard dimly, but distinctly, in the Allied camp miles away above the Valley of Balaclava.

Lord Raglan, general-in-chief of the British Expeditionary Army, sighed on the camp bed in his house. He was old, he was overworked, ill and weary; the stump of his right arm—amputated at Waterloo 40 years before—was giving him pain. Lord Raglan's mind, none too keen to begin with, had been growing increasingly cloudy. The Crimean conflict was his first taste of war since the days of Napoleon and, although the French were now his allies, there were moments when he thought he was fighting them, and not the Russians.

He was more than inefficient—he was incompetent. But no one thought of removing him or of asking him to resign. He was more than just an officer and a gentleman. He was Field Marshal the Lord Fitzroy James Henry Somerset, Baron Raglan. He was a Peer of the Realm. He was an aristocrat.

A voice was heard in the dark distance. Then another, nearer. Another, still nearer. The sentries were crying the "All's Well," as they did every half hour to show they were not asleep. The horses moved restlessly, then quieted. The sick and dying lay on the ground, thin blankets over them, nothing under them. As the effects of opium and rum, the only medication given them for cholera, wore off, they vomited, groaned, raved in delirium.

From the tent of the Cavalry Division's commander, Lord Lucan, came loud snores. He was 54 and needed all the sleep he could get, because the whole division would be awakened an hour before dawn, as always.

No one had ever accused Lord Lucan of being either intelligent or kind-hearted. In the year of the Great Famine he had evicted 50,000 starving tenants in Ireland, pulled down their cottages to prevent them from returning, and then locked the doors of the poorhouse. He was not likely to lose rest over a few hundred dying enlisted men. Prior to the Crimea, he had not seen any military action in 26 years—but he was also a Peer of the Realm and an aristocrat.

Not far off was the bell-tent of the C.O. of the Light Brigade. But the tent was empty. The C.O. was 67 years old, his bladder bothered him, and so did his bowels; salt pork, biscuit, and watered rum—the usual military fare in the Crimea, owing to a complete foul-up in the matter of supplies—did not agree with him. Furthermore, he detested life in the cold, muddy, bug-ridden camp, so he slept on his own private yacht, *Dryad*, in Balaclava harbor. There he was tenderly tended by his steward, valet, and cook. The harbor was several miles from the camp and the C.O. did not believe in hurrying his horse or in getting up early. Accordingly, he arrived hours late every single morning.

He, too, was a Peer of the Realm and an aristocrat. He was Major-General the Earl of Cardigan, Lord James Thomas Brudenell, Commanding Officer of the Light Brigade, and so—although he was a fool, a martinet, and a monomaniac—he could do just about as he damned well pleased.

A keen commentator on the military scene said of all three lords—Raglan, Lucan, and Cardigan—that they were "absolutely unfit for the positions they had secured through family and political influence . . . Had they been privates, I don't think any colonel would have made them corporals!"

And while the struggle for the great Russian Black Sea naval base at Sebastopol went on amidst death and agony in the south-west Crimea, the British High Command there had a little war of its own going on, for Lord Cardigan was not on speaking terms with Lord Lucan and Lord Lucan was not speaking to Lord Raglan. Cardigan wrote long letters to Raglan complaining about Lucan. Lucan wrote long letters to Raglan complaining about Raglan *and* Cardigan. Raglan (who had no time for long letters) wrote notes to both Lucan and Cardigan. One of the notes was to produce the most famous cavalry charge in history—a charge which was technically not a charge at all. That note also was to destroy the flower of the British forces, take hundreds of lives, and produce a poor poem whose rushing lines remain in the mind when better ones have left it. This is the note:

Lord Raglan wishes the cavalry to advance rapidly to the front, follow the enemy and try to prevent the enemy carrying away the guns. IMMEDIATE.

Which "front?" Which "enemy?" Which "guns?" Why? Where? How?

Not only did the 17th Lancers, the 4th and 13th Dragoons, the 8th and 11th Hussars—making up the Light Brigade—not only did *they* wonder, but in a short time *"All the world wondered."* However—

> *Theirs not to reason why,*
> *Theirs but to do and die.*
> *Into the Valley of Death,*
> *Rode the six hundred.*

But all this occurred later in the day. Now, it was still dark.

The commandant at the Port of Balaclava could not sleep. The cries of the sentries and the ice-cold wind howling down from Central Asia were not the only things disturbing him. He had a lamp, pen, ink, and paper brought, and he sat down to write a communiqué to Lord Raglan. He wished to remind the general-in-chief that he had had no reply to his earlier notification that a Turkish spy had reported massive Russian troop movements toward Balaclava from the east. The British position was now merely untenable—if the Russians succeeded in cutting the main supply lines, it would become impossible.

The commandant sighed, and laid down his pen. It was useless. Lord Raglan had been warned and had done nothing. He notoriously did not like to be bothered by details, and his aides —including five of his nephews—were all devoid of military experience.

Through the cracks in the windows came the stench that was Balaclava—dead men, dead mules, dead horses, camels and oxen; spoiled and rotting supplies; dung, sewage, vomit, and long-unwashed men. The commandant winced, blew out the lamp, and returned to bed.

About an hour later a glow, like that of sunrise but from the opposite direction, was observed. It came from Sebastopol. Flames, started by the previous day's bombardment and kept under control until now, had gotten out of hand. Encouraged by this, the French artillery at once began to fire. The British camp awoke and cursed. Red and yellow flashes lit up the night, and the smell of gunpowder soon overwhelmed all other smells.

Old Lord Raglan cried out in his sleep. In an instant his chief of staff, General Airey (age 51; military experience, none) was at his side.

"M'lord?"

"Whose heavy guns are those firing?"

"M'lord, the French."

"We must attack them immediately!"

General Airey had to remind him, yet another time, that the French were no longer "the enemy." Finally the old man got it into his weary, fuddled head where he was, and why. Groaning weakly, he tried to get some more sleep.

Lord Lucan bounded out of the sack at the first cannonade. "What's the time?" he demanded.

"A little more than an hour before dawn, my lord."

"Mmph. Have the men stand by their horses."

The cavalrymen, stiff with cold, staggered up from the iron-hard ground, saddled their mounts, and fed them from the scant rations. They crammed some dry biscuit into their mouths, and were standing—gummy-eyed but at attention—when Lord Lucan cantered by in the darkness on the day's first inspection tour.

The siege-guns roared from the batteries—Lancasters (the first rifled ordinance—and none too dependable, either), 32-pounders, 68-pounders, mortars, and 24-pound rockets. The artillery had been shelling Sebastopol for over a week, all day long and every day. It intended to go on doing so until the Russian base surrendered. Or until the Allied forces were obliged by lack of men or supplies to lift the siege.

Meanwhile, on his luxuriously-fitted yacht in the harbor, Lord Cardigan continued to sleep, a silk-slipped and down-stuffed pillow under one ear, and a second pillow over the other ear to keep out the noise. Siege-guns were no business of his. His business was to see that the Light Brigade of Cavalry was in tiptop shape, and to lead it into battle (and glory) when the proper time came. Dawn, in the opinion of the major-general, the Earl of Cardigan, was not the proper time.

The earl's second-in-command, Lord George Paget, was trotting around the camp with Lord Lucan. Gradually the blackness gave way to grayness. The siege-guns paused. It was a heavy, overcast day. Morning mists lay heavily in the valley and along the ridge. Slowly, the thick gray cloud rolled back. Suddenly there was another peal of artillery.

"Hul-lo. That's not siege-guns."

"No, Lord Lucan. Those are the Navy 12-pounders we brought up to the redoubts and turned over to the Turks."

"The Turks! Well, what are *they* up to?"

Lord George took a good look. "They are flying two flags at their signal-staff, sir."

"Two?" Lucan stroked his mustache. "That means, 'Enemy approaching,' " he said calmly. Obligingly, at that moment the mists rolled further away. In a flat, harsh voice, Lucan said,

"Damn—my eyes!" Advancing down the valley below in two immense and heavy columns was what seemed like the whole Russian Army —infantry, cavalry, artillery. Battalion after battalion, in long, belted gray coats and flat-topped hats, bayonets fixed; cavalry with drawn swords and readied lances, and horse-drawn cannon by the score.

The Turkish spy, it seemed, had been right after all.

"There must be at least ten to twenty thousand of them!" the younger man exclaimed. And added, tactlessly, "I wish Lord Cardigan were already here."

Lord Lucan's port-colored cheeks went purple. He thrust out his lower jaw in a horrible grimace. "Cardigan!" he rasped the hated name. "He is never where I want him to be! Damn him! Damn him!"

At just about this moment, down on his yacht, Cardigan himself arose, took a cold tub-bath, carefully brushed and combed his blond mustache, thinning hair, and long side-whiskers, had some breakfast while his valet laid out the clothes, and then dressed. The regiment of which he was colonel (as well as being the brigadier of the whole Light Cavalry) was the 11th Hussars. It was their uniform he was wearing—royal blue pelisse with gold lace and gold braid, cherry-red trousers with gold stripes, fur shako with white plume. His orderly was waiting on the pier with a splendid chestnut charger, Cardigan's own mount, Ronald.

Some time between eight and nine the noble lord and general began his ride toward camp. His pace, as usual, was leisurely and he paid absolutely no attention to the men galloping past him, nor to the noise of the conflict raging up ahead. For some time he said absolutely nothing. Then he commented, in his hoarse voice, "Wretched country, this."

"Yes, my lord."

"Wretched country. No game at all!"

What sort of person was this Earl of Cardigan, soon to be the most famous—or most infamous—man in Britain? Those who knew him expressed different opinions. "The entire Army does not contain a greater muff or a more dangerous fool," said one. "A braver soldier never held a sword," said another. The truth seems to be that both were right.

He was "the handsomest man in Europe . . . a splendid, glossy animal . . . uncertain and violent of temper . . . did not know what fear was . . . harsh and domineering . . . mediaeval and chivalrous . . . uncontrollable and subject to fits of extraordinary and unreasonable rage . . ." The writer of these last lines, Cecil Woodham-Smith (whose book, *The Reason Why*, is the authoritative one on the subject), summed it up by saying of Lord Cardigan, "The melancholy truth was that his glorious golden head had nothing in it."

And what little there was in it was permanently disordered when, in teen-age, the "glorious golden head" was kicked by a horse. But it all made no difference. He was a noble lord, immensely wealthy, indulged by doting parents, and spoiled by a total of six loving—and lovely—sisters. Only one thing was he denied—participation in the Napoleonic Wars. He was an only son, and his parents would not risk it.

Cardigan had been living ever since for the chance to make up for the fact that glory in war had been denied him in his youth.

At the age of 26, Cardigan fell in love. He had not been idle until then; far from it. Scores of bastard children were attributed to him. If this seems unlikely to us, it must be remembered that he was rich, he was noble, handsome, heedless, and passionate— and he lived at a time when birth control was almost unknown. The woman he now fell in love with was married to his good friend, Captain Johnstone. This made no difference to the lord, who eloped with her.

Captain Johnstone described her as "the most damned bad-tempered and extravagant bitch in the kingdom"—and happily sued for divorce, and got it. It was only a short time before the lady's second husband came to agree whole-heartedly with her first. They parted, but there was no divorce. Lord Cardigan had joined the Army.

Among his fellow-officers was a dark, dashing, handsome young lieutenant-colonel, who soon proceeded to marry Cardigan's favorite sister, Anne. She eventually left her husband. There had never been any love lost between the two brothers-in-law. Now, intense dislike broke out into active hate.

Lord Cardigan's brother-in-law was no smarter than he was, but he was Cardigan's senior in rank. He remained so. His name was Lord Lucan, and he was Lord Cardigan's immediate superior on that day at Balaclava so many years later.

Cardigan was mad for speed; today, probably, he would be racing sport cars. He did the best he could do in his own period. He joined the cavalry.

How did an officer of the British Army advance in rank in those days? Influence, that is, "pull," counted heavily, to be sure; but the chief means of advancement was simply money. Incredible as it may seem today, from 1683 to 1870, if an officer in the British Army wanted a commission, he had to pay for it. *He simply bought his rank as he might buy a house, a horse, or a yacht.* Men with no money were kept out by this system, of course, but then that was the whole idea. Men without money were too apt to have radical ideas.

Neither Lord Lucan nor Cardigan had any radical ideas. In fact, they had scarcely any ideas at all. Their chief conviction, the principal one animating the life of each, was that he was a king of creation and his personal whims and crochets had the force of natural law. Lord Lucan, in 1826, wanted the command of the 17th Lancers. He got it—for £25,000 [about $125,000]. Lord Cardigan, in 1832, desired the lieutenant-colonelcy of the 15th Hussars. For a mere $175,000, it was his.

The 15th Hussars were a crack regiment, but Cardigan wanted them to be more, much more, than that. He stopped at nothing. All night drills, all day field-days, courts-martial, punishments, forced resignations—it became an open scandal. It even reached the editorial pages of the influential London *Times*, which called the noble Lord "an unripe gallant . . . a man of no experience . . . incapacitated for command by temper [and] by ignorance, [who] ought never to have been placed at the head of a regiment."

Result: "His Majesty has been pleased to order that Lt. Col. Lord Brudenell [Cardigan] shall be removed from the command of the 15th Hussars."

Two years later, Lt. Col. Childers of the 11th Light Dragoons (Hussars) put his commission up for sale. Lord Cardigan promptly bought it, for $200,000, and the same business began all over again. He had an almost insane demand for perfection. Horses, men, officers, all had to meet that demand—or break. Many broke. One soldier who had attracted his displeasure was flogged on Easter Sunday after church let out. The 11th Hussar's C.O. was hissed and booed in public. He didn't give a damn.

Slowly but certainly he beat the 11th Hussars into the sharp shape he wanted them. Grim, stone-headed, ruthless, kindly only to women, he waited for war. He was determined that when it—and the chance for glory—came, he and his hussars would be ready for it.

And in 1854, the chance came.

Since the days of Peter the Great the Russians had been seeking a so-called "warm-weather port," that is, one which would not freeze their navy in the ice for half the year. They also intended to carve a huge slice out of European Turkey, which then comprised all of the Balkans north of Greece. Czar Nicholas I began his plan by building a huge naval base at Sebastopol, in the Crimea, on the Black Sea. Britain and France watched uneasily.

In 1853, war broke out between Russia and Turkey. The czar's forces invaded the Balkans and destroyed the Turkish fleet. If the Russians once succeeded in establishing themselves in the Mediterranean, not only would the balance of power be thrown up for grabs, but the British "lifeline" (via Suez) to India, Australia, and the Orient would be imperiled. In March 1854, Great Britain and France declared war on Russia. An expedition of both nations, plus the Turks, was planned to the Black Sea.

The officials of Her Majesty's Government, civilian and military, were unanimous in their belief that the best man to conquer the Russians was the one who had been the Duke of Wellington's right-hand man for 40 years, to wit: Lord Raglan. Hadn't he lost an arm at Waterloo? What more could one want? The expeditionary army was to consist of six divisions, and command of the Cavalry Division was given to Lord Lucan.

The cavalry was divided into two brigades, heavy and light. The Heavy Brigade went to a General Scarlett, and the Light Brigade to General the Earl of Cardigan, who marked his appointment by issuing two orders. Order Number One: All swords to be sharpened. Order Number Two: Leather insets to be sewn into the seats of all trousers . . .

"British cavalry officers," observed a marshal of the French Army, "seem to be impressed by the conviction that they can dash or ride over everything . . . precisely the same as in foxhunting."

This was certainly true of Lord Cardigan. In addition, he was impressed by another thing; that his subordination to Lord Lucan was purely nominal, and that the Light Brigade would operate as if there was no one between himself and Lord Raglan. Raglan seemed to support this view. No one bothered to consult Lord Lucan.

As a result, Lucan did not catch up with what was, after all his own command for months. He arrived in Turkey—Cardigan had gone to Varna in Bulgaria and taken the cavalry with him. Lucan went to Varna, only to find that Cardigan had moved on to Devna; so had the cavalry. By the time the cavalry's official commander got to Devna, Cardigan had taken off to Yeni-Bazaar with the Light Brigade.

Why did the general-in-chief allow all this? Simply because Lord Raglan, stupid as he was, had sense enough to realize he had to keep the two brothers-in-law apart.

To everyone's surprise, the Russians retreated from Bulgaria. What to do next? It was up to Lord Raglan to pick the place to fight. And, by and by, Lord Raglan picked it.

With almost no supply lines, he decided to cross the Black Sea, invade the Crimea, and capture Sebastopol.

As one officer wrote in his diary, *"The taking of the place is impossible, and the plan is that of a madman!"*

The voyage from Bulgaria to the Crimea should have taken three days. It took 17. Cholera broke out aboard the transports. The dead were too many to allow canvas shrouds, so weights were tied to their feet and over the sides they went. The weights were heavy enough to keep the corpses upright, but not heavy enough to pull them under. A long line of rotting, grinning heads marked the passage of the Allied troops across the Black Sea. It was an omen.

An unopposed landing was made at the tiny port of Balaclava, south of Sebastopol. The whole campaign was a hideous farce. The Allies won victories, but failed to follow them up. At one point the Russians in Sebastopol were sure they could not hold out against an attack, but the attack was never made. The men went hungry, the horses ate their own ropes. The troops died of cholera, they died of dysentery, they died of typhus.

And Lord Cardigan continued to ignore his frenzied brother-in-law.

Lucan, finally, insisted upon exercising his command in full. Lord Raglan gave way. Cardigan continued as before. It was now Raglan's turn to be fed up. Cardigan was told, abruptly, to straighten up and fly right. Henceforth, he was to obey Lord Lucan—promptly and in all things. Cardigan reacted with the sullen passion of a spoiled child. "Promptly and in all things," eh? *Very* well. So be it. He would obey every damned order. And if the orders should be wrong—even if they should be obviously and shamefully wrong—he would be damned if he'd point this out; no, he would *obey*.

This was how matters stood on the morning of October 25, 1854.

The Valley of Balaclava lies several miles above the harbor, and is about three miles long. Within the valley itself, which runs roughly east-west, are considerable differences in elevation. At the western end are hills known as the Heights, where Lord Raglan had his headquarters. A ridge called the Causeway bisects the terrain lengthwise into the North Valley and South Valley. The northern one is about a mile wide, bounded on the south by Causeway ridge and on the north by the Fedukhine Hills. Along the ridge ran the so-called Vorontsov Road.

This road formed the only decent supply line between Balaclava harbor and the Allied lines besieging Sebastopol. It was the purpose of General Liprandi, the Russian C.O., to cut this line. It was the purpose of Raglan—insofar as his tired, old mind still had any purpose—to prevent his doing so.

Along the Causeway were six redoubts, or emplacements—two north of Vorontsov Road and four south of it—containing all told nine 12-pounder naval guns with Turkish crews. The Light Brigade was stationed at the far western end of the North Valley.

While Lord Cardigan was jogging leisurely up from the harbor, the Russians attacked vigorously from the eastern end of the North Valley. Redoubt Number One resisted, but was overwhelmed. Redoubt Number Two hardly bothered to resist, and the men in Numbers Three and Four did not bother to resist at all, but got the hell out as fast as they could. The Russians demolished Redoubt Number Four near the Allied lines, but occupied the first three.

It was about 9:30 in the morning when this phase was finished, and at this moment up rode Lord Cardigan. Also riding in was another mass of Czarist troops, who proceeded to occupy the Fedukhine Hills with both infantry and artillery. The besiegers, outflanked and surprised, were about to become the besieged.

"Lord George Paget," said Cardigan, coming up to his second-in-command; "I now relieve you."

"Very good, my lord," said Paget. He was a colonel in rank. Cardigan passed within a few feet of Lucan. Neither looked at, nor spoke to, the other.

From his position on the Heights, Lord Raglan had a perfect

view. The last traces of mist and cloud had vanished and the air was unusually clear. Thus, when several thousand Russian cavalry began advancing up the valley toward the Allies, Raglan could see them plainly. Owing to the rises and dips in the valley itself, however, the British troops below could not see this new movement.

(There was no semaphore system or telegraph line set up.) The two cavalry brigades continued to sit calmly on their mounts, yawning, smoking, and scratching themselves. Only 200 yards now separated the two forces.

Raglan, 700 feet above, went pale. The stump of his right arm jerked and twitched. Then, abruptly, the Russians turned left and began to pass over the Causeway ridge into South Valley.

The Argyll and Sutherland Highlanders, like all other regiments, had been decimated by disease. There were only 550 of them at the moment when the 4,000 Russian cavalrymen approached at a right angle. "Form in two lines," directed their commanding officer. "No retreat—we must die where we stand."

The Highlanders nodded grimly and—with fierce Gaelic shouts—charged the astounded enemy.

The Russian advance stopped dead. The Czar's troops were not expecting any attack from that quarter—certainly not one in skirts! The "thin red line of heroes" fired three volleys. The Russians, suspecting an ambush, turned and fled.

All talk ceased among the Light Brigade as they heard the sound of the Minié bullets. "Hullo!" cried Cardigan, wheeling his horse Ronald around. "Hul-lo! Enemy approaching? Ha! Paget, they shall have to order us to charge!" Forty-odd years he had waited—and now the chance had come! A *charge*!

The pictures of Cardigan at this period give a first impression of foppishness. This is due to the dandyish uniform, to the heavy side-whiskers framing the smooth-shaven chin, the hand on hip. But there is nothing of the fop or dandy about the firmness of that chin, the stubborn out-thrust of the lower lip, the arrogant curve of the nostril, and—above all—the cold, determined stare.

It was probably true that "his mind was petrified by 30 years of peace-time service," and that he was "arrogant, supercilious, selfish, and hated by his men." But he was not a coward.

It was still not Cardigan's moment. In fact, it was not yet the Light Brigade's moment. The enemy, routed by so small a group of Scots that the Russians later were incredulous, now came surging forward upon an even smaller force—500 men, of the Heavy Brigade, under General the Honorable James Scarlett.

Scarlett had never come within range of anything larger than a kettle-drum before in his life. Now he saw what seemed like endless lines of enemy lances framed against the sky over the hill facing him. He did not hesitate.

"Heavy Dragoons, wheel into line!" he directed as the Russian cavalry poured over the crest of the hill. "Prepare to charge!"

The Light Brigade was 500 yards away, Cardigan, seeing Lord Lucan coming toward him at the gallop, drew himself up firmly.

To Cardigan's rage and chagrin, Lucan said, "Hold your position here! On no account leave it! Attack whatever comes within reach of you!" And with that, he galloped away, shouting for Scarlett to charge.

The trumpet, sounded. The Heavy Dragoons rushed upon the enemy, Scarlett 50 yards in front of his squadrons. There was no space to level carbines; the two forces fell upon each other with cold steel, as if gunpowder had never been invented. Red coats and gray, screaming horses, shouting men—the struggle raged under Cardigan's nose while he rode back and forth in front of his brigade, loudly and hoarsely complaining, "Oh, those damned 'Heavies!' They'll have the laugh on us today!"

Then, for the second time that morning, the impossible came to pass. The Russians faltered—paused—fell back—turned—and retreated. The Heavy Brigade cheered, reformed their ranks, but didn't pursue. Cardigan sat glowering on his horse, gnawing his mustache. "Hold your position here—" Wasn't that what Lucan had said? Damn him! And, "On no account leave it?" Very well, so be it. Stupid order, but—he would obey it and, if Lord Raglan didn't like that, well, let him blame Lucan!

Meanwhile, Lord Raglan, upon the Heights, swept the valley ceaselessly with his field glasses. He sighted in on the Causeway ridge, near the Russian-captured redoubts, and saw teams of horses, lasso tackle . . . His satisfied smile vanished. "The guns—the guns—the naval guns!" he cried. "They are going to haul the guns away!"

Instantly, his 50 years' obsession—"enemy-French"—leaped into his mind, as vigorously as ever. "They mustn't! The Duke of Wellington never lost a gun to the French! What will the French think, if we lose our guns?" The guns were already "lost," of course, but to see them actually hauled away— "An order to Lord Lucan!"

His chief of staff, General Airey, came running up. Raglan, twitching and trembling, dictated.

Lord Raglan wishes the Cavalry to advance rapidly to the front— follow the enemy and try to prevent the enemy carrying away the guns . . . Immediate.

And so, with 25 words, he condemned the Light Brigade to death . . .

Captain the Honorable Somerset Calthorpe—one of old Raglan's innumerable nephews—an officer detached from the Light Brigade's Eighth Hussars, had the aide-to-camp duty. But he was passed over, and a Capt. Lewis Nolan singled out to carry the message. As Nolan vaulted into the saddle Lord Raglan called to him, "Tell Lord Lucan the cavalry is to attack *immediately*!"

Who was Nolan? He was—or fancied he was—a cavalry expert. Most of his experience had been with the Austrian cavalry, in which horses were taught such tricks as walking on their hind legs. Paget called him "reckless, unconciliatory, and headstrong." But then Paget, like almost all the Cavalry Division, hated him—for Nolan had been loud in his contempt for the stodgy British horse-troops. He called Lord Lucan, "Lord Look-On," and everyone knew it. Including Lucan.

To have chosen Nolan over the more level-headed (and popular) Calthorpe was a fatal mistake.

As Nolan tore into the cavalry camp, Cardigan looked up, and broke his silence. "Who is that, my lord?" he asked Paget. Lord George told him, adding, "A great man in his own estimation."

Lucan received Nolan coldly, read the message slowly. Then he read it again, with increasing bafflement and irritation. "Advance rapidly to the front—" Raglan hadn't said *which* front. "Follow the enemy—" Follow *what* enemy? "Try to prevent the enemy from carrying away the guns—" *What* guns? Lucan did not know what the hell Raglan was talking about.

Lucan did not know, because he could *not* know. Lord Raglan, 700 feet above the valley, could look down on the Causeway ridge. But Lucan, who was *below* the ridge, could not possibly see what was going on among its dips and folds. Raglan had had clear evidence of this when the Russian cavalry had approached unobserved, *but he had already forgotten it!*

Nolan was almost dancing with impatience. Lucan shook his head. There was only one thing to do—admit ignorance and inquire of the commander's messenger what the commander had intended the message to mean.

Nolan, it now seems probable, *did not know what guns were meant, and did not know that he did not know!* He threw out his hand toward the only artillery in sight, the great double batteries at the far end of the valley, and in a loud, excited, insolent tone, he half-shouted, "*there* is your enemy, my lord! *There* are your guns! And *there*—" gesturing toward the message, "*There* are your orders!"

If Lucan had been a more sensible man he would have spoken calmly to Nolan, attempted to reconstruct the scene at headquarters, and the conversation there, as well. This might have done the trick. But Lucan was an arrogant blockhead; all he knew was what the regulations said that a general's orders, when brought by an aide-de-camp, had to be obeyed as if delivered by the general in person.

He shrugged, and rode off to Lord Cardigan.

Nolan, who was panting for a chance at a charge himself, then approached a captain of the 17th Lancers. "Sir, we are to attack. May I ride with your squadron?" Permission was granted.

Cardigan stared at his superior with his cold, blue eyes. Here, again, the sensible thing was for Lucan to consult with his second-in-command; to show the order and ask for an opinion. But of course he did not do so. He had hated Cardigan's guts for years. And the man had defied him, had tried to run an independent command earlier in the war. No, Lucan would not *ask* his hated brother-in-law anything.

"Lord Cardigan, you will take the Light Brigade and advance toward the enemy at the end of the valley. I shall follow with the Heavy Brigade. We are to try to prevent the enemy carrying away the guns."

Cardigan saluted with his sword. Here was the chance for which he had waited 30 years! And yet—a fool he might be, but somewhere a small grain of common sense now made itself felt. "Allow me to point out to you, sir," he said, in a voice neatly balanced between respect and contempt, "that the Russians have artillery and riflemen in front and on both sides."

Lucan gave him stare for stare. "Those are Lord Raglan's orders," he said. "Advance steadily. Keep your men well in hand." Cardigan again brought his sword to the salute; then both men rode off.

As Cardigan did so, he was heard to say, "Well, here goes the last of the Brudenells!"—his family name. To Paget he said, "Lord George, we are ordered to make an attack to the front. You will take command of the second line, and I expect your best support —mind, your best support."

Cardigan galloped off and formed the Light Brigade into two lines—first, the 13th Light Dragoons, 11th Hussars, and 17th Lancers; second line, the 4th Light Dragoons and the 8th Hussars. To none of the regimental commanders did he condescend to say a single word.

As a final touch, Lord Lucan now detached the 11th Hussars

(Cardigan's own outfit) from the front line and formed it into the second line of the Light Brigade; thus turning the original second into a third line. Cardigan then rode five lengths (about 40 yards) ahead of the first line. He tightened his sword belt, drew his sword and held it out, point downward. A trumpet sounded.

As calmly as if he were on a paradeground, he said, in a hoarse, quiet voice, "The Light Brigade will now advance. Walk! March! Trot!" In unison the three lines of the Light Brigade moved off down the Valley of Balaclava. There were exactly 660 horsemen.

To the left of them were 14 cannons, 4 cavalry squadrons, and 8 infantry regiments armed with rifles. To the right of them were 11 infantry battalions, a field battery, and 30 cannons.

In front of them were 12 or 18 cannons, 6 squadrons of Russian lancers, and almost 10,000 cavalry.

So struck by astonishment at this insane advance were they, that the Russians did not fire a single shot. Their entire lines fell utterly silent and through the North Valley of Balaclava no sound was heard but the thud-thud of the Light Brigade's horses' hooves on the turf, the words of command, and the jingling of harness-bits and sabers.

The brigade advanced 10 yards—30 yards—50. At this moment Captain Nolan, riding with the 17th Lancers, must have suddenly realized that they were advancing in the wrong direction. His face twisted with horror, he spurred his horse, pointed his sword to the right (toward the redoubts), shouted at the top of his voice as he galloped across Lord Cardigan's path. ("Second squad, three *right!*" cried a captain of Lancers.)

Cardigan did not, then or after, turn his head an inch—

"How dare you!" he cried to Nolan. "Get away, damn you! Get back!" And it was exactly then that the Russians began to fire.

A shell fragment tore open the left side of Nolan's chest so that his heart lay bare. He dropped his sword (though not his sword arm, which stayed raised) and gave a most terrible scream as his horse carried him, erect, past the whole first line—the horrified men could plainly see the heart still beating—then it ceased to beat—and Nolan fell dead from his horse. ("Second squad, threes *left!*" the captain of Lancers shouted.)

From the Fedukhine Hills on the left, from the Causeway heights on the right, from the end of the valley up ahead, shell-fire and rifle-fire poured into the three beautifully straight, gorgeously uniformed lines. And still Cardigan kept them down to a trot. Any faster pace, he felt, would lack dignity.

The C.O. of the 17th Lancers increased his speed to a canter, which brought him abreast of Cardigan. "My lord, this is a murderous fire!" he cried. "Let us get to the guns as quickly as possible!"

Cardigan whipped his sword against the officer's chest. "Do not ride level with your commanding officer, sir. And don't force the pace!"

The captain dropped back, but his men had already anticipated an increase in speed, and Cardigan's keen ear caught their quickened motion. "Steady, steady, the 17th Lancers!" he cried, hoarsely. Obediently, they resumed the trot.

A round-shot bounded along the ground right in front of him, spraying dirt in his face. Undaunted, he took a reading on the guns ahead of him, sighted in on the flash of the central cannon, and rode straight for it without flinching, faltering, or slouching. The men behind him could hardly do less. He never ordered the "Charge" to be blown, and by this time it would have been too late, as all three trumpeters were down. The astonishing fact thus is, that *the Light Brigade never actually charged at all!* It "advanced!" As the

> *Cannon to right of them,*
> *Cannon to left of them,*
> *Cannon in front of them*
> *Volleyed and thundered;*

And as man after man and horse after horse went down—dead, shattered, wounded, bleeding—those still mounted were obliged to expand their ranks to avoid trampling, as well as stumbling. Immediately after each such expansion, the lines contracted. With the perfect precision which Cardigan and

Lucan had beaten into them year after year, the ranks—ever pressing forward—went *out* and *in* and *out* and *in*. And with each *in* the brigade grew smaller. The effect was weird and wonderful and—to those who watched from above—utterly heartbreaking.

One sergeant "rode fully 50 yards with his head shot off, his horse keeping its place in line." The Light Brigade rode right on. "Round-shot, grapeshot, and shells began to mow men down, not singly but in groups; the pace quickened, and quickened again . . . and the trot became a canter." So C. Woodham-Smith described the scene in *The Reason Why*.

And, meanwhile, what of Lord Lucan? "I shall follow with the Heavy Brigade," he had told Cardigan—and follow he did—up to the point where the crossfire began. An aide killed, himself and horse wounded, Lucan finally came to the abrupt conclusion that:

Someone had blundered!

"They have sacrificed the Light Brigade!" he cried. "But they shall not have the Heavy, if I can help it—Sound 'Halt!'" And that was as far as they went.

The French *Chasseurs d'Afrique*, deciding to aid the Light Brigade's return, did what Lucan didn't; charged the Russians in the Fedukhine Hills, and routed them. The Lights would now face fire from one side less when it returned.

If it returned.

At three-quarters of a mile, and the same distance to go, the canter became a controlled gallop. The beautifully dressed lines began to change position. "Come on!" the men cheered, over the noise of artillery, the scream of shells, the whistle of Minié bullets. "Come on! Come on!" And, crying, "You bastards won't stay ahead of *us*!" the Fourth Light Dragoons left the third line and caught up with the second. With the breath of the first line's horses hot upon his neck, Cardigan laid his heels into Ronald's sides. Erect and unwavering, he sped right for the flash of the center cannon of the enemy's double battery, and his men came swiftly after him, cheering, shouting, and dying.

And still the awesome discipline kept up. "Close in, there!

Dress up those lines!"—lines growing thinner with every pace
—"Right flank, keep back! Left squadron, close in to your center!
Close in!"

Only eight minutes had passed since the "Advance" was
sounded. The brigade, or what was left of it, was now close
enough to see the frenzied faces of the Russian gunners. Cardigan now selected a space between the two centermost guns and
rode straight for it, flourishing his sword. Twenty yards—ten
yards—eight—would *nothing* stop these madmen? The Russians
fired one last, tremendous salvo straight into the British ranks.
The 17th Lancers and the 13th Light Dragoons were wiped from
the face of the earth.

At that moment the Light Brigade as a unit came to an end.

Cardigan and horse were lifted off the ground in a burst of
flame, and then dropped. Straight into the smoke they charged,
first to enter the enemy ranks. The 37 survivors of the 17th and
the 13 survivors of the 13th forged in behind him, slashing with
their sabres at the artillerymen, who were trying to remove their
cannons.

"Where are you all going?" Cardigan cried, not slackening his
pace. "Rally! Rally to me!" He vanished into the smoke.

Behind him a Lancer called to his mate, "General says, 'Rally to
him!'"

"*What*? And be made cold meat of? No, no—keep to bloody
hell away from that mad old bugger—"

Sweating, screaming, gorgeous uniforms covered with dust,
the Fourth Light Dragoons galloped in next and completed the
capture of the guns, and pressed in after Lord Cardigan. After
them came the 11th Hussars on the left flank and the Eighth
Hussars on the right flank. Cossacks charged them and were
driven back, Russian Lancers charged them and were driven
back . . .

"Where is Lord Cardigan?" the officers yelled. "Has anyone
seen him?"

But Cardigan did not hear them. Deafened, first by the guns,
then by the sudden silence, he had galloped right through the

battery to come face to face with about 3,000 Russian cavalry-men. Without a moment's hesitation, and as if the same number of British were right behind him, he charged them. It had been a day of great surprises for the Russian forces, and by this time they no longer knew *what* to expect of the mad English. As the noble and half-cracked earl, sunlight glittering on his sword, gold braid, and gold lace, came dashing at them, hell-for-leather, they gave way in confusion.

Among their officers was a Polish prince who had spent some time in England, where he had attended all the cavalry reviews. Now, to his astonishment, he recognized that unforgettable English cavalry officer, Milord Cardigan. Prudently spurring his horse out of the way, the prince shouted to the Cossacks, "Take him alive!"

The contest was scarcely an equal one, and after a few minutes of parry-thrust-slash, Cardigan was wounded. This convinced him; he began to fight his way *out*, instead of *in*. In another few minutes he stood beside the now-deserted guns, and found himself alone. Some of his men, finding it impossible to remove the guns to the British lines, had disabled and over-turned all they could; then retreated. Others, having flanked the battery, and observing that no support (such as the Heavy Brigade) was on hand, had also decided to return.

Cardigan knew nothing of this; the terrain prevented his seeing much. So, displaying the same iron nerve as during the advance, he now made his way back.

He bore a charmed life, for as he rode untouched down the center of the valley, remnants of his brigade were making their way back along the two sides. There was no longer any fire from the French-captured Fedukhine Hills, but a ceaseless and merciless rain of shot continued to pour down from the Causeway ridge.

Wounded men slumped in their saddles; wounded and unwounded men slowly walked back, tenderly leading wounded horse; some staggered in, clutching shattered and bleeding flesh; some rode piggyback on unhurt companions. There was no such thing as line, regiment, or squadron now, no cheers or trumpets —only the fire from those same guns on the Causeway which Lord Raglan had been so sure the Russians were going to remove.

Six hundred and sixty Light Brigaders had ridden down *Into the Valley of Death* (Tennyson had the wrong figures). One hundred and ninety mounted men answered to the roll-call. One hundred and thirteen were known killed, 134 were wounded. Of the rest, some had returned dismounted, more had been captured by the Russians, others were simply "never seen again."

"Men," said Cardigan, in his husky voice; "it was a harebrained trick, but it is no fault of mine."

"Never mind, my lord," a man cried; "we are ready to go again!"

Cardigan, characteristically, did not reply to this voice from the ranks.

Some distance away, face livid and drawn, Lord Lucan stood. Their glances met. Neither one said anything. After all, they were not on speaking terms.

Down from the Heights came old Lord Raglan, head trembling, the stump of his right arm jerking. In a quivering voice he demanded of Cardigan "what he meant by attacking a battery in front, contrary to all the usages of war?"

Cardigan, savoring the moment, calmly answered, "I received the order to attack from my superior officer, my lord." And that was that. Raglan rode away. All afternoon the survivors of "The Charge of the Light Brigade" sat slumped in their saddles, waiting for orders which never came. Flasks circulated, and they all proceeded to get quietly drunk. They deserved it. It was past midnight before they were allowed to turn in, without fires or food. Long before then, of course, Lord Cardigan had returned to his yacht, taken a warm bath, dined on game pie and grilled ham, drunk a bottle of champagne, and turned in between the silk sheets of his bed. He slept like a baby. So ended the day for which he had waited all his life.

Less than two months later he applied for a medical discharge, got it, and returned to England to find himself a hero.

THE MEN WHO KILLED THE BRIGADE

The crowds which had hissed him, now kissed him. The Queen sent for him, he was made inspector-general of cavalry, and half the hairs were pulled from poor Ronald's tail for souvenirs. The noble earl lapped it up. From his speeches one might have assumed that he charged the Russians all by himself.

But *someone* had to be blamed, of course. The choice was not long in coming. Lucan told the truth—it was Raglan's fault. But the government wouldn't buy it. "It is felt that the public service and the general discipline of the army renders Lord Lucan's withdrawal in all respects advisable," ran the order. "It is Her Majesty's pleasure that he should resign the command of the Cavalry Division and return forthwith to England."

He demanded a court-martial. He didn't get it. Cardigan's triumph was now sweetened by his enemy's disgrace. It didn't stay sweet for long. Returning veterans of the Crimea were quick to complain about his status as chief hero. Why hadn't he looked around during the "charge" and seen that he was not heading for the *right* guns (i.e. the ones in the redoubts)? Why had he abandoned his brigade after reaching the *wrong* guns? Why had he so neglected the brigade's subsequent welfare that half the survivors died the winter following? Why—

He was snug in his yacht while his men had scarcely any clothing to cover their nakedness, swarming with lice, very little rations, dying in their tents of hunger, wet, and cold, and everyone suffering with disease and no medicine to give them, not even clean water to drink . . ."—Why?

Raglan died of a broken heart, but it was just not in Cardigan to blame himself for anything. He considered handing out challenges again, then decided to celebrate the peace with Russia by remarrying, instead. The duels might have been preferable, after all. The second Lady Cardigan was a lulu—did Spanish dances at the dinner table, went bicycling in her husband's old Hussar uniform, and threw the crockery at His Lordship whenever the tizzies took her. The Hero of Balaclava was soon a nervous wreck, had a stroke in 1868 while horseback-riding, died.

Lord Lucan outlived him till 1888; in fact, Lucan outlived all his enemies—except for a few inlisted men, and they didn't count.

The historic "Charge" had a curious and little-known effect on our own history, too, for the American military observer in the Crimean War was Captain (later General) George McClellan. "It is difficult to divine how such a charge could have been ordered by any officer," he wrote. "Destruction was inevitable. One arm of the service may occasionally be required to sacrifice itself for the benefit of the others, but this was not such a case; it was an exhibition of insane and useless valor . . ."

When "Little Mac" was head of the Union Army he applied the lesson he had learned from Balaclava, and it was this; Caution —caution—caution. Before Lincoln fired him, it almost won the Rebels the war.

Many useful reforms were brought about, however, by the follies of the Crimean War. Military hospitals became vastly improved, for example, and commission-by-purchase was outlawed. A tiny handful of Light Brigade survivors lingered on into the early 20th century. The British Government was not unmindful of their gallantry and sacrifice, their secure place in poetry and history. It allowed each man the magnificent pension of . . . a shilling [about 25 cents] a day!

LITTLE RENÉ

I N FEBRUARY, 1958, in the sun-baked desert town of Lucerne Valley, California, a gnarled little man was found dead of a heart attack. His name was René Belbenoit and his death was duly noted by the nation's press because Belbenoit once had been something of a celebrity. But a few lines of cold type couldn't begin to do justice to the story of this man—an epic of human suffering and survival that has rarely been equaled. Because of him the worst prison in modern times has been destroyed. This is his story.

It will be a long time before the ghosts stop haunting French Guiana, before the newest *departement* of Metropolitan France can forget the 50,000 tortured souls whose lives were claimed by the "Green Hell" in the days when it was a penal colony. If it can ever forget.

The French Government promised $50,000,000 to "rehabilitate" its only mainland possession in the Western Hemisphere. The penitentiary in Cayenne was to be torn down, Isle St. Joseph was to be converted into a resort and Isle Royale into a seaport; roads were to be built and large scale mining and agricultural projects begun. France and her South American colony wanted to forget the 50,000 dead convicts—dead of overwork, of malnutrition, of every tropical disease from malaria to leprosy, "shot while trying to escape," buried one atop the other in the overcrowded graveyard, or thrown to the sharks—forget them. Why not? France had forgotten them while they were still alive. But one man had kept reminding them.

René Belbenoit . . .

In 1923 Belbenoit was just one of 700 prisoners lined up in columns of four in the great stone-paved courtyard in the St. Martin de Ré prison. At a barked command they marched forward between a double line of fixed bayonets, the wooden soles of their jail shoes clattering awkwardly. The annual convict ship was in port at La Rochelle. France's chief export to her oldest colony—French Guiana—was being readied.

"Don't try to escape," barked a guard. "Don't be in any hurry to die. Half of you will be dead within a year, anyway!"

"Half?" an old convict from the African military prisons growled out of the corner of his mouth. "Three-fourths is more like it."

The man next to him, clad in gray woolens too big for him, winced. René Belbenoit was only 21, tiny and slender, with a puzzled expression in his unusually large eyes—eyes that were to see much in the next 14 years, and to forget nothing. But in 1923 he was just another convict. That he was a disabled war veteran meant nothing. That his bungling theft, committed when out of work and hungry, had been of a necklace worth less than $300, and that he had been promptly caught, also meant nothing. That is, not quite nothing; it meant that the odds against his surviving his five-year sentence were not good.

In the gray September drizzle they marched aboard the prison-ship and were stowed away in its iron cages. Only a handful of them were ever to see France again. Gradually the air in the stinking hold grew hotter. Then on the fourteenth morning the engines stopped. Belbenoit, straining his eyes toward the dirty porthole, saw the yellow-brown stain of the Maroni River, and then the green mass of the jungle.

Two hours later they were in the rotting little town of St. Laurent, distributing center for prisoners. Marching down the sunbaked streets splattered with the gray droppings of innumerable vultures, the convicts looked across the river. On the opposite bank was a village, neat and white. *Dutch Guiana! Freedom! Escape!*

And then they saw the high, bleak walls of their destination. Over the great iron gates was painted "CAMP DE LA TRANS-PORTATION, For The Expiation Of Crime, The Regeneration Of The Guilty, And The Protection Of Society." Fancy words! Society would, perhaps, be protected. Beyond doubt the crime would be expiated. But almost never would the guilty be regenerated. René was to learn, soon enough, that the system was not aimed at reforming the convicts, but at killing them off. The gates closed . . .

Belbenoit and a dozen others were pushed into the large cell which they were to share with an equal number of old-timers. Hoots and whistles arose from these last, and cries of "New blood!," "Fresh meat!"—and others, unprintable. They gathered around to see if they knew any of the newcomers. One of them shambled up to René.

After a single glance and a shake of his scabby head, he said, in a not unkindly voice, "All right, chicken. Those three planks there—that's your bed." René took in the yellow eyes, sunken and gray-stubbled cheeks, toothless mouth. Was this how he would look in a few years' time—if he lived? Speaking half to himself, he said, "So this is Devil's Island?"

The old man gave a ghostly chuckle. "Ever since Dreyfus' time the world thinks the whole colony is Devil's Island. No. chicken, that's only for political prisoners. But if you stay here long enough you'll get to stay at the other islands—St. Joseph and Royale. So don't despair of seeing the Devil, because he's here, all right."

Finally night came. The men were shackled to their beds by one ankle, and René fell into a shallow sleep. France . . . Paris . . . the night club where he'd worked before World War I. He was awakened by a terrible scream. Opposite him one of the newcomers threshed against the confining shackle, trying to kick something off the imprisoned foot. Something black. Finally an old-timer, with a curse, threw his tin bowl. The black thing dislodged itself, vanished into the blackness of the night on fluttering membranes of wings.

"Only a vampire bat," muttered a veteran. "You'll get used to them."

But the days were worse than the nights. Breakfast was a cup of coffee, dinner was a piece of bread and a piece of meat, supper was a cup of beans or rice. At least on paper. Actually graft reduced even this meager ration. The guards stole part of what the Administration hadn't stolen, and the turnkeys and cooks —themselves convicts—stole part of the rest. The meat was mostly gristle, the rice and beans, mostly moldy and weevilly. Graft was the axis on which the Colony revolved. No one had taken a job for the sake of lightening the burden of the convicts. The civil employees stole to make money, the convicts stole to be able to escape, to add to their "salary" of 10 centimes—two cents —a day. Out of this they had to pay for tobacco, soap, writing paper, stamps.

Small wonder the strong stole from the physically weak, or that the morally weak succumbed to the almost universal vice, becoming the *môme*, or sweetheart, of older and stronger convicts. Belbenoit, whose sharp eyes missed little, noted the rarity of really veteran convicts. "Every year 700 new men arrive," he wrote in the record he had begun to keep, and out of which three books were to grow; "and yet the total number does not increase. When a convoy comes in the total rises to 3,500, but in the time before the next shipload the count has dropped to 2,800 again . . ." It was a neat equation: 700 arrive—700 die.

Famished, weak from loss of blood because of the vampire bats, feebled by hookworm, dysentery, and a hundred other diseases, the men toiled in the burning sun or in the fetid jungle. Heat prostration carried them off. Venomous insects and snakes attacked them. They cut down the iron-hard trees of the Guiana jungle, pulling the logs with ropes that ate into their flesh and produced sores which soon infected.

And the guards, well-fed, puffing pipes, lounged in the shade, rifles under arms, and growled at the naked, fainting men. "First one that stops work stops a bullet!" Literate France allowed them not a single book, Catholic France allowed them not a single priest. In the dry season the sun burned them. In the wet season the rains drowned them. At night the prisoners, barefooted, filed back to their cells, pausing to raise their hands so that the turn-keys could frisk them.

Belbenoit's weight dropped to below 100 pounds. His teeth fell out from scurvy. Only one word kept him alive. Escape!

The tool of escape, in French Guiana, was not the file, but the *plan*. A *plan* is a capsule, usually of aluminum, with blunted point at each end. It screws into two pieces. Inside can be folded up to eight bills of any denomination. Where is a convict to get money, so that his *plan* can become, as they say, "charged"—so he can buy supplies for escape? If he has anyone in France, money can be sent via a guard, who keeps not less than half as his cut. If not, he saves his 10 centimes daily pay, and gambles at cards. If he loses, he carves souvenirs to be sold to the few tourists. He catches butterflies, whose wings are worth a few francs. He finds a graft of his own—gives up smoking, sells his tobacco at a small profit and steals supplies, if he can wangle access to them.

If all else fails, he finds another convict who has money—and kills him for it.

Where does he hide his money? In the safest place he has—his own body. The *plan*, in short, is a suppository.

"What's the best way to escape?" René began asking the older convicts.

"Bribe your way into being sent to Cayenne," one told him. "It's right on the ocean. You get a boat and then you have your choice: Brazil is south, Venezuela is west, the islands are north. You can make a deal with a fishing-boat to smuggle you out."

Another warned, with a grimace, "And once he's got you at sea, he knocks you on the head, cuts you open for your *plan*, and throws you to the sharks!"

"Right here in St. Laurent is best," said a third. "The river takes you into the sea, doesn't it? Only watch out for that spot just above the wrecked ship—the current will turn you over in a second." And then, excited, as always, by the mere thought of escape, the conversation became eager. "You need five hundred francs—less won't do." "Give a black fifty francs to ferry you in his canoe over into Dutch Guiana—then stow away on any ship!" "Watch out for the mudbanks at Nickery—the Dutch call it 'The Frenchmen's Grave!'" "Up the Mana River into Brazil—that's best!"

Franc by painful franc Belbenoit added to his little hoard, and word by agonized word he added to his written record. And then, suddenly, fortune smiled on him. The French authorities in Guiana had always been leery of journalists, lest they expose the horrors of the convict colony, and the graft which was its mainstay. But in 1927, when Belbenoit's sentence still had a year to run, two Americans managed to slip past the watchful eye of authority, and visit St. Laurent. One was the architect, Robert Niles, the other was his wife, Blair Niles, a well-known writer.

"If I can only get to see them . . ." René murmured. He was working at the sawmill then. The hardwood resisted the edges of the revolving blade. The convict next to him slipped, cursed— then screamed as he fell upon the whirling saw. In the ensuing excitement, René stole away.

"But if you have only one year more to serve, why do you want to risk escape?" Mrs. Niles asked him, having carefully locked the door.

René made a gesture of despair. "Ah, Madame—you don't know about the terrible system of *doublage*? It works like this: After the sentence is over, the 'liberated' man is not allowed to return to France—or to anywhere else. *He must remain in French Guiana for a time equal to the length of the time he has already served!* And if his sentence was for more than eight years, then he must remain here for life! Legally, he is free. Free to starve! Madame Niles, there are no jobs to be had. The colony's only industry is the convict settlement—all the work is done by convicts. Do you know why there are no dogs on the streets? The *libérés* eat them! Here they say 'The real punishment begins when the convict is liberated.'"

Blair Niles realized, then, that the gaunt, furtive men skulking and begging in the streets, were not convicts, but *liberés*—"free men!" She took the pages René had copied from his record, and gave him several hundred francs. "We are going into Dutch Guiana next week," she said. "Then to the States. If I find your writings can be used, I'll be in touch with you again."

Belbenoit walked away on air. He had more than the necessary 500 francs, now. It was August 10th. He would escape within a week, meet the Niles in the Dutch Colony, and implore their help in getting on a ship. Finally, he made his plans. His companion in the escape was to be Leonce, a young convict who was anxious to get out of reach of the tough, homosexual prisoners.

August 14th was the day set. It was Queen Wilhelmina's birthday, and the Dutch colony would be too busy celebrating to be on the lookout for escapees. For provisions, Belbenoit wrote later, they had "bread, sardines, condensed milk, salt, tobacco, and a bottle of matches." They crept away from the camp and floated across the Maroni on a raft, hastily put together, which had been hidden in the underbrush.

Once on the other shore, they plunged into the jungle. Accompanied by the weird cries of howler monkeys, terrified by a six-foot poisonous bushmaster serpent, they made their way through the tangled underbrush. Gold birds whistled, macaws squawkled, parakeets and frogs added to the chorus. This racket continued, in slightly different keys, throughout the night, and into the next day. Then they made the mistake of stumbling into a clearing where some Carib Indians were at work. The red men dropped their hoes, seized their weapons . . .

"Papers?" asked the Dutch official. The two stricken young Frenchmen patted their clothes, muttered something about having lost their documents. The Hollander sighed. "There was a time," he said, "when you poor devils were safe here. But not long ago one of you killed a merchant in Paramaribo. Our first murder in almost a hundred years. Since then we have orders to send you back. Sorry." Stunned, they mechanically took the cigarettes he offered.

Belbenoit's first escape had lasted all of 36 hours!

The guard who marched them into the disciplinary block-houses gestured to five flat white stones set into the yard. "That's where the widow with the sharp tongue stands," he sneered, referring to the guillotine. "So take care!" He kicked them into a cell crowded with 50 other men, all shackled and awaiting trial. No smoking, no card-playing, no ten centimes a day. Just wait-ing. Wrote Belbenoit, "All the men were naked, having bartered their clothes for tobacco . . . the irons clicked and rattled with in-cessant monotony . . ."

Since this was his first escape, the Special Maritime Tribunal gave René a light sentence: 60 days in solitary, then to Camp Nouveau. When released, he was too weak to stand, and his feet were so infested with chiggers that he couldn't walk. He had only a pair of rotting shorts for clothes, and there were none to issue him, for a crooked official had sold the clothing to gold miners. He wrote, "There are 400 men in Camp Nouveau, includ-ing 100 who are blind—amputees—deformed—elephantiasis— etc. *None are excused work . . .*"

Before long he stood before the Commandant on charges: "Belbenoit, Number 46,635, reported himself sick twelve times after drinking his morning coffee."

"Belbenoit," said the commandant, "you were not too sick to drink the coffee, eh? Four days in cell on each of the first six charges, eight days for the next three, fifteen for the next two, and thirty for the last. Maybe a hundred and eight days will cure you of your taste for coffee, eh?"

A hundred and eight days convinced him only that it was better to lie in the cell than to die of overwork or sunstroke, and on his release he frankly told the Chief Guard so. The Chief wanted no trouble. "Look, Belbenoit," he said. "I will give you a good racket: infirmary attendant. You see in my garden, there, the trees? Orange and chestnut. You sell the fruit and nuts to the patients. The oranges are my cut, and the chestnuts are yours. Content?"

Content, René sold roasted chestnuts. He also sold tobacco, rum, and bread. He also sold the medical supplies. "It is every man for himself," he wrote; "and if I don't, another will. And I need the money for my next escape." Four months later, on Christmas Day, he and eight others were at sea in a dugout canoe. The water barrel had, with hideous appropriateness, formerly served as barracks chamber pot. Life in *La Bagne* had cured the men of any fastidious feelings. Most of the money had gone for food—coffee, rice, bananas, canned milk, dried beef. The canoe had cost them not a *sou*, they had stolen it from a Chinaman.

Big, tough, tattooed Marseilles was at the helm. But they had Basque, a real sailor on board, and they had let him come for nothing, to navigate. Big waves blew up, began to drench the pirogue. "Come up and take over, Basque," said Marseilles, scared.

But Basque was more scared. "I lied!" he whimpered. "I can't steer or sail! I had no money to put in—so I lied. *Forgive me!*" But there was no pardon. Basque, who had periled their lives, was thrown to the sharks. The canoe wrecked upon the coast of Dutch Guiana. And then began a march of horror. Food gave out. Peg-legged Gypsy killed little Robert for his can of milk. Marseilles killed Gypsy, and the starving men then grilled his liver and ate it. Wrote Belbenoit, with numbed detachment: ". . . the fire was kindled with Gypsy's wooden leg!"

A few days later they were recaptured and sent back to St. Laurent. So ended Belbenoit's second escape. He paid little attention when the Tribunal classed him as "Incorrigible," and gave him six months for the escape, plus another six months for insulting a doctor who had refused him hospital care.

The first six months he served in one of the "death camps"—Charvein—working in ankle-deep mud. His feet ulcerated. For the second six he was sent to Isle St. Joseph, where were located the cells for "reclusion"—solitary confinement—of incorrigibles. "My jaws clacked with fever," he wrote, "I vomited constantly." Released, he was sent to the notorious *Case Rouge*—

Red Barracks—on Isle Royale, named from the great number of murders which occurred there.

Belbenoit now weighed about 80 pounds. The doctor, an Army surgeon named Rousseau, took one look at him, and ordered chicken soup. The Chief Guard guffawed. Chicken soup for a convict! As it happened, this man owned the only chickens on the island. A few moments later the noise of rifle-fire was heard. The guards turned pale. Prison break? No—only Dr. Rousseau shooting the Chief Guard's poultry! Belbenoit got his soup, it saved his life, but Dr. Rousseau was sent back to France.

Restored to health, René wrote, "Well did Victor Hugo call this penal settlement '*dry guillotine?*' Who will write its terrible story, its own *Les Miserables*?" Back in the United States Blair Niles had written her *Condemned To Devil's Island*, based on the accounts Belbenoit had given her.

And then there was Josette.

It had been years since René had known a woman, years since he had more than dared *look* at a woman—at the guards' wives, the fat tarts, the Creole girls. Josette's father, a guard, hired Belbenoit to tutor her in preparation for entering the high school in Cayenne. In short time the precocious Josette had begun to tutor René. The affair between the 16-year-old and the young convict not yet 30 bloomed with tropical rapidity.

Of course they were found out, René was returned to Isle St. Joseph.

His spirit too subdued for further resistance, René finished his time and was returned to the mainland. Blair Niles sent him money. In a short time he was over into Dutch Guiana again. This time he thought to travel only by night, but he was caught anyway. To another jungle death camp, then again to the islands —the dreadful cycle began all over again. This time it was to Camp Kourou that he was sent, to labor on the infamous "Route Zero"—the road which went from nowhere to nowhere, and in 25 years had not even reached a length of 25 kilometers. Its only purpose was to kill off troublesome convicts.

It failed to kill Belbenoit. He was sent back to St. Joseph, and from there to the penitentiary in Cayenne. And there Governor Siadous heard of him, and sent for him.

The French rotated their colonial governors every two years. If any administrator had any ideas of reforming Guiana—and few did—they had barely time to begin before their term was over. To Belbenoit's complete astonishment, he learned that Governor Siadous did have exactly that idea in mind—and that he wanted his assistance! "You write, one hears—and you expose the corruption which runs on here," Siadous said. "Well—write for me!" René obeyed.

His fingers flew, the brief notes were expanded. There wasn't a racket, a crooked guard, he didn't have the goods on, nor a previously-hidden act of cruelty he didn't point out. All this was to do him no good later on, but at the time he thought nothing of that. He had the Governor's good will, didn't he?

The Governor read the report, re-read it, had it copied. "Perhaps this will do some good back in France," he said. "I hope so . . . I will do my best."

And then one morning, the cell-keeper doling out the coffee said to René, "Tomorrow you will have to earn this." His sentence had finally expired, he was now a *liberé*. As a result of seven years of labor, minus deductions, he was awarded the sum of 85 francs; and was informed he was forbidden to live in Cayenne, and—of course—could not leave the Colony itself. But the Governor thought differently.

"You have money, Belbenoit, from Mme. Niles, from her book? Over twelve thousand francs? That should be enough for a while. I, too, have something for you." And he handed him a paper.

"DECREE OF THE GOVERNOR OF GUIANA. . . That the *liberé* René Belbenoit, *Liberé* Number 36,444, is authorized and given a passport to leave the colony for one year.

Cayenne, 27th September, 1930

SIADOUS, Governor"

Through a mist of tears Belbenoit read the words. "I have faith in you," the Governor said. "Do not fail to return. Prove that a *libéré* can be trusted, and we will be able to do the same with others. Good luck."

Feeling as if he were dreaming, René took passage on the ship *Biskra*, bound for Panama. Only one incident marred the trip. Two guards on leave, not knowing of his status, ran up to him shouting, "Belbenoit, you aren't getting away with it!" But their smiles of cruel triumph changed to chagrin when the purser pronounced his documents in order. That night, just for spite, he sat at the table next to the guards and ordered champagne!

The Panama Canal Zone authorities allowed Belbenoit to stay, on condition he find work within a month. Blair Niles wrote to Governor Burgess, who got him a job as gardener at Gorgas Hospital on Balboa Heights. Here he was happy. On the night side of town he soon made the acquaintance of other Frenchmen, many of them Guiana escapees.

But time was running out for Belbenoit. His passport and parole would expire on November 12, and it was now October. He had given his word not to escape. Was there an alternative? Two things tipped the scale against his return to Guiana. One was that the Chamber of Deputies had voted unanimously to repeal *doublage*. The other was the news that his one ally in the Colony, Governor Siadous, has been transferred to the Orient. Without him, Belbenoit well knew, his career in Guiana wasn't worth mud.

On October 19 he stowed away on the French Liner *Wyoming*, bound for Le Havre. The first day out, he surrendered himself. "What's your idea?" the ship's officials asked, more curious than angry.

"If I get to France before my passport expires," René explained, "they can't charge me with having violated my parole. If the Senate confirms the Chamber's vote, I can stay in France. If not, at least I can apply for a Presidential pardon. When we get into Le Havre I want the police to come aboard for me. That way no one can say I was caught on land while trying to escape."

Brave plans! The *Wyoming* docked on November 2, 10 days

before his passport ran out. The police took him ashore. The Magistrate gave him two months for stowing away, and sent to Paris for further instructions. He was allowed to make an immediate application for a pardon to the Ministry of Justice. On December 31 it was returned to him with one word written across it: *Rejected!*

He was moved to a Central Prison and put in solitary. It was bitter cold and he was barefoot; his blood had been thinned by the tropics, but he had enough practice enduring solitude. He kept walking round and round his cell, wrapped in a single blanket. After 30 days he was transferred to the same prison from which he had left for Guiana nine years ago, St. Martin de Ré. To the other convicts awaiting transportation, he was living proof that escape was possible.

"It's easy, isn't it?" they asked him. He shrugged. They would find out soon enough. Of the 700 men who had gone out with him, only 15 were still alive in Guiana. Of those who had escaped, most had died before reaching freedom.

One day he was summoned to the office of the tough Corsican warden, who was crimson with rage. "So this is how you expect to get a pardon, is it?" he shouted, slamming his fist down on an open copy of the *Police Magazine*. Dumbfounded, René learned that the magazine had only now begun printing a series of articles he had sent from Guiana when he was Governor Siadous' white-haired boy, and felt safe. "To the cells with him," the warden yelled. "Fifteen days—bread and water!"

The French writer, Francis Carco, observed him after his return from solitary, although René didn't know this till later. Carco wrote, "The man walked with lowered head . . . He seemed puny and suffering. His uniform was too large and he had to turn the sleeves back. Belbenoit was back in the rounds again and only he, at the price of a thousand stratagems, could get himself out again. In the stupefied line of marching men he walked mechanically. Around the court and around again without end, abused, washed out, overcome . . ."

On September 20th, exactly 10 years after his first trip, he trudged aboard the same convict-transport bound once more for the Green Hell, the Dry Guillotine. He was a marked man. When the men in his cage complained about the food, the captain had René shackled to the bars by both ankles. "But," as he wrote, "I had lived through Hell before."

And, flat on his back, "puny and suffering," he talked again of escape. "The blacks and Indians in Dutch Guiana get five francs a head for each escapee they catch," he cautioned the others; "and they're liable to kill you for your *plan* . . . It might be wiser to try Brazil . . . beyond the Tumuc-Humac Mountains you'd be safe . . ."

Once again the prison depot at St. Laurent gave Belbenoit its grim welcome. "The Chief Guard caught my eye. 'Belbenoit—to the Blockhouse!' he barked. And he added mockingly, 'You know the way.' So my convict life began anew."

Public Prosecutor Barbet glared at him. "The Special Maritime Tribunal will try your case," he snapped.

"For what?"

"Escape."

"But I had permission—a passport—it's in the records—"

"Tell it to the judges!"

And then Barbet waved the *Police Magazine* at him, wrathfully. "You'll pay dearly for these!" he shouted.

René's letters to the Governor and the Attorney-General were stopped by the Penal Administration. The guards stomped on his bare feet with their heavy shoes. He knew he had to get to the Governor before the Tribunal acted, but the Governor was in Cayenne. Therefore, he had to get to Cayenne. If not by one way, then by another. So he sent word to St. Germain, Commandant of the St. Laurent prison, that he had a message for him—important and confidential. St. Germain doubtless hated and despised the tiny, toothless convict—still—down he came, uniform, ribbons, gold-braid, and chicken-guts.

"You have something to tell me, Belbenoit?"

"*Oui, mon Commandant*—" Then, at the top of his voice: "You're a lousy S.O.B.!"

Scarlet with rage, St. Germain shouted, "In irons!" His order was promptly carried out, not gently. But Rene, by now, was used to pain "as a familiar companion." His scheme was this: Having insulted a high Administration figure, he would be brought before the Court of Correction. Since he was still a *liberé*, he had the right to appeal the decision, whatever it was, to the High Court in Cayenne . . . where the Governor was.

From the familiar cramped and stinking cell, the equally familiar and constricting irons, he was half-marched, half-dragged to the Court of Correction.

"Belbenoit, *Liberé* Number 36,444 . . . One month in the Blockhouses."

Number 36,444 said, "I demand my right to appeal to Cayenne!"

An angry, then a cunning look, came over Prosecutor Barbet's face. "Oh, you can appeal," he said; "—but not till I'm good and ready to let you. Till then—" He jerked his thumb and they frogwalked René back to the upright coffin of his cell.

"*That night*," wrote Belbenoit, "*my love for France died within me.* That night I set myself to live only for escape, that I might write a book which would help destroy Devil's Island and all that the name stood for."

Finally the Special Maritime Tribunal convened. The little wisp of a prisoner was guarded by a squad of huge, black Senegalese soldiers.

"We, Lamy, Governor of Guiana, by virtue of the rights conferred upon us, order for trial *Liberé* Number 36,444, Belbenoit, René, accused of breach of residence under the provisions of Article 6, of the Law of May 30, 1854." The court was jammed with Penal Administration figures, come to see this buzzing little bug crushed forever. On the bench in scarlet robes, the President of the Tribunal put his face through a constant series of grimaces which were tactfully ignored until a month later, when he was declared insane.

In vain Belbenoit insisted that he was not only innocent, but that his very indictment was illegal. The prisoner has no rights which the jailer is bound to respect. Prosecutor Barbet outdid himself. "Belbenoit *is* guilty!" he shouted. "Belbenoit is to be convicted! If he is given only two years, the two years spent in jail after his apprehension will be counted, and he will go free tomorrow. I demand the maximum sentence—three years at hard labor!" The courtroom burst into applause.

Belbenoit's "lawyer," a green young guard, got up and in a trembling, weak voice, quavered, "I ask the indulgence of the Court for my client"—and dropped into his seat! Twitching, the President found René guilty and gave him the three years demanded. René was, however, allowed a formal appeal to Paris, and a letter to a lawyer in France. He selected the famous criminal advocate, Maître Rouvières. But both letters had to go through Barbet, and he held back the one to the lawyer for two months.

Well before then, of course, the appeal was heard by the Court of Criminal Appeals in Paris. It chose to dispose of 200 cases in two hours' time, and so Belbenoit received about 90 seconds' attention. Verdict? "Case in order. Sentence legally pronounced. Appeal rejected."

It was now April, 1934. In Guiana the triumphant Commandant twisted his mustache like a silent movie villain, and said, smugly, "Well, Belbenoit, you won the first round—but you've lost the second. Inscribe him on the convict rolls again," he directed; "then put him in solitary. He goes to the Islands on the next boat . . ."

Waiting for him on Isle Royale was none other than the guard who'd tried to arrest him on the *Biskra*, on the way to Panama. "Well, Belbenoit," he greeted him balefully, "here you don't buy champagne—Frisk him well and take him to the *Case Rouge!*" In the old "Blood Barracks" René found something new had been added: machine guns.

The C. O. was a bad sort, but not such a bad sort for a bad sort. "You dumb —, you should've stayed in Panama," he said, staring down curiously at the diminutive convict, in red-striped uniform and wide straw hat too big for him. "And you shouldn't have written those — articles. I'll give you a break: You can have the job of sweeping the courtyard."

This time René kept his nose clean, and was presently returned to the mainland. By 1935, with his "liberation" close at hand, he began making plans to escape once more. He was deluged with requests to "take me with you, I'll pay all expenses," but—warned by previous bitter experience—preferred to take his time and select his getaway mates with caution. No more murderers or false "navigators!"

He first accepted Casquette, a *liberé* who fished for sea-turtles in an Indian pirogue which he kept concealed on the Isle of Lepers. "Three men came to meet us," René wrote of his visit to see the boat. "One had no hands . . . just hanging claws! Another had his body covered with bandages soaked in yellow pus. The third one had no nose . . . Among the 70-odd men standing around [I saw] faces eaten away, enormous ears, stumps of arms and legs . . ." And the Fatherland of Pasteur allowed these men to rot —they were merely convicts—without a single doctor!

The canoe seemed all right. For René now a *liberé* again, the chief problem was money. There was none to be made in town, so he turned to the forest. "There in that rain-soaked jungle which the condemned curse," he wrote, "God has put a brilliant thing, resplendent and fragile, to help the miserable men conquer their freedom." With desperate zeal Belbenoit hunted butterflies—the Caligo, Morphos, Rathenor, the Achilles, the Papillo and the Laranta Fulgens—blue, mauve, green and gold; their wings worth from six to 40 francs.

As the money gradually mounted, he picked his other mates: Dadar, a first-offense burglar—Bébert, four years in solitary for hitting a guard—Panama, caught after 12 years' freedom, and Chifflot. No one was interested in Chifflot's crime, he could sail, that was enough. There were new difficulties now in the way of escape which had not existed in René's early day. Neither Colombia nor Venezuela would now accept escapees. And the Administration had a new patrol boat, with high-powered lamps and mounted machine guns.

At six o'clock in the evening, May 2, 1935, Belbenoit and his six companions set off on his fifth escape. Situated so close to the equator, Guiana has no dusk to speak of. Almost at once it changed from day to dark. Slipping down the Maroni toward the ocean, they crouched low, and to the occasional hail from a canoe of Indians or Bush-Negroes, they made no reply. When the sea began to breach over them, they knew they were safe from the patrol boat.

"Hoist sail," directed Belbenoit. A patchwork sheet made of hammock and old clothes was raised.

"Chifflot, take the tiller. The rest—bail."

All the men had agreed to follow René's orders, but just in case —he had a tiny pistol, wrapped in oilcloth, inside his shirt. It had also been agreed that Trinidad, 800 miles away, was to be their destination. Oddly enough, this British island had originally been closed to escapees, but when the Latin American republics followed suit, the chivalrous Trinidadians agreed to allow escapees to land, though not to stay.

The men in the tiny vessel—three feet wide—were constantly wet. The sun beat down until its glare almost blinded them. Their skin cracked open. The salt water swelled up their old ankle-sores. By the fourteenth day their supplies were running out. Mutiny threatened. "We'll never get to Trinidad," Dadar swore. And Bébert urged making for the coast of the mainland and risking capture. René pulled his gun out. And then, with melodramatic suddenness, Chifflot sighted Trinidad! They had made it!

The six scarecrows staggered ashore, to the terror of the local Negroes, who nevertheless gave them coconuts. The sweet milk tasted like nectar to Belbenoit, who wrote that "the earth seemed to dance under my feet, to ebb and flow." After a while they felt strong enough to totter along to the nearest police station, to claim refuge.

The constable of Noruga village was a vast Negro in a spic-and-span white uniform. He ordered his policeman to "get eighteen loaves of bread, six pounds of rice, six of sugar, six of coffee, six of codfish, and twelve packs of cigarettes." Before they could arrive an old black woman cooked them a meal. Belbenoit could always taste it, afterwards, and remember each item; rice, baked plantains, fresh fish, hot coffee, mango preserve and salt beef. She refused pay.

"The law of Trinidad is," said the huge constable, "that if your boat is not seaworthy, you may stay until other transportation is arranged."

They drove back to the beach. The Trinidadian looked at the tiny craft, already splitting apart, then at the sea. He shook his head. "You go to Port of Spain."

In Port of Spain, the island's capital, Captain and Mrs. Heap of the Salvation Army took them in and served them another meal. Casquette and Bébert, who had not sat at a table in 15 years, wept. Chifflot now revealed that he had 4,000 francs in a *plan*, and proceeded to buy a fake Venezuelan passport and a ticket to Hamburg, from there to sneak into France. And the others?

An answer was supplied by the Inspector-General of Police. "Giving you a boat," he said, with affected brusqueness. "Make up a list of supplies." His eye fell upon the bulky, oilcloth-wrapped package under Belbenoit's arm. "What's that?"

René explained it was the record he had been keeping for years, managing—somehow—to avoid its confiscation. "I will write a book," he said, "which will expose the rottenness of the Guiana convict system. It will kill Devil's Island!"

"Mmph. Badly needs killing," said the Inspector. "Best of luck."

A Navy launch towed them past the dangerous waters of Dragon's Mouth, and finally, 10 miles out, let go. The five men in the sailboat waved thanks, and headed for Panama. Sixteen days later they were wrecked off Colombia, on the desert coast of Guajira, and were robbed by the Cactus-Eater Indians of everything but the machete. With this they killed and ate iguanas and frogs. They staggered along, naked and blistering, on festered feet.

When they broke into a hut which contained nothing but

dresses, they were glad to put them on. A few days later they hit civilization, were arrested by laughing soldiers, who paraded them—shaking with fever—through a mob of jeering people and barking dogs. The C.O. sent for quinine, food, and clothes; then got down to business. The next day they were in Baranquilla, Colombia, in prison, waiting for next month's French ship to return them to the Green Hell once more.

Belbenoit escaped.

He made his way, on foot, past Cartagena and toward the Panama border. There, in a jungle hut, he met the legendary Ensign Gautier, himself an escapee. René stayed four months, hunting butterflies, and made $100. Then he pushed off again. All along the Panama Coast and among the San Blas Islands he used the same technique: Each night he would creep up to a sleeping Indian village and steal a canoe. Each day he would beach it and proceed afoot. He did this 20 times.

Finally he came to rest among the Chakoi, a tribe of northern Panama, and here he remained seven months, recuperating in the hut supplied him by his native "wife." She was a plump, comely young squaw, with but one flaw: she couldn't cook! So René himself fixed the wild rice and venison, the sweet potatoes, squash, and corn.

Panama—Costa Rica—Nicaragua—robbed by bandits—up and down mountains—jailed—released—Honduras—through ravines—along mule trails—San Salvador—warned against Guatemala: new dictator.

He decided, in the port of La Libertad, to stow away aboard a ship said to be bound for Mexico—or was it Canada? Either one, René felt, would do. From either he could make his way into the United States. He hid in the rope-locker. After his own food and water were gone, he stole that set out for the ship's dog! He lost track of the time. Finally the ship stopped.

Timidly, he peered out. Mountains reared against the skyline. On the dock two men in strange uniform frisked each sailor who went down the gangplank. *But they didn't ask for identification!* Putting on a brave front, René walked down. The men patted

him, glanced at his bulky package, waved him on. He was ashore
—but what shore was it? He came up to a group of men languidly
repairing street-car tracks.

"Where do these tracks go?" he asked. They stared at him.

"To Los Angeles, you dope!" one of them said.

René Belbenoit thanked him, then, as he later wrote, "I walked
off with a springing step. I was terribly emaciated. I had no
teeth. I had one pair of cotton pants. One cotton shirt. One hand-
made cotton coat. A pair of ragged shoes. That was all I possessed. *But I was no longer afraid.* I entered the outskirts of Los
Angeles as happy as a lark."

With his 30 pounds of manuscript René made his way to New
York. "I will wait and see what will happen to me," he said. What
happened to him was good—at first. E. P. Dutton brought out
his book, *Dry Guillotine*, and it hit the world like a blow. Edition
followed edition. It went into cheap reprints and was condensed
for the *Reader's Digest*. *Newsweek* wrote, "Fifteen years of tropical sun and jungle-fever have done their work. His teeth are
gone and his eyesight, nearly; he weighs well under 100 pounds.
Burned a deep leather color, he looks half again his 38 years.
[If] he will be sent back to Guiana, his punishment will be five
years in solitary confinement on the Isle Royale, in other words
—death . . . His *Dry Guillotine* is one of the great documents of
prison life."

The eyes of the world were turned on France, to see what her
reply would be. Her first reply was to ban the showing of the
Warner Brothers moving picture, *Escape From Devil's Island*. But
the arrow had sunk home. No more convicts, it was announced,
would be sent to Guiana. As for those there—as for the *liberés*—?

In 1939 René was ordered to leave the United States. Friends
urged him to take another name, move. "This country has been
good to me and I will not be dishonest with it," he said. It was
the old story of his word of honor to Governor Siadous, all over
again. But this time he avoided France! He went to Mexico, but
was ordered out. He retraced his steps through Central America
to Panama. But he found he couldn't stay, he had to return to the

United States, come what may. Like any wetback, he swam the Rio Grande.

"The alien, Belbenoit—no number: Illegal entry. Penalty: Fifteen months jail."

But to a veteran of Devil's Island, an American Federal Penitentiary was like a resort. He emerged, cheerful and chipper, tried to enlist in the Army. Needless to say, he was rejected as several times 4F. Not even the Immigration Authorities had the heart to suggest he be deported to German-occupied France. Let alone to Guiana, where a Vichyite Penal Administrator had filled his empty cells with Gaulleists, and where conditions were more brutal and cruel than ever.

At the turn of 40, after years without family, Belbenoit wooed and won an American wife. Now, at last, he experienced the joys of marriage and fatherhood. But deportation and French prison —somewhere—always threatened.

Undaunted, he brought out his second book, *Hell On Trial*, in which he dealt with individual cases of injustice and corruption—naming names and fearing nothing. Finally, World War II was over. And finally—90 years after its founding—the prison colony at French Guiana was abolished. The penitentiary at Cayenne was torn down. A new Governor, Jean Prevet, had agreed to serve a 10-year term to see the reforms carried through. And the Salvation Army took back to France every *liberé* who wished to leave.

But—though acknowledging Belbenoit's role in bringing this about—France issued no pardon. "The man who killed Devil's Island" was still an escaped convict to his native land. And hourly facing deportation from his adopted land.

In 1947, at the eleventh hour, a bill was introduced to Congress, entitled simply, H.R. 4,485, "A Bill For The Relief Of René Belbenoit. Be it enacted by the Senate and House of Representatives of the United States in Congress assembled, that notwithstanding any provision of the immigration laws to the contrary, the alien René Belbenoit should be permitted to remain in the United States for permanent residence."

It was so enacted.

Forever gone, now, was the fear of the felon's cell, the shackles. After 24 years, René Belbenoit could feel himself perfectly free and perfectly safe. He left his job with the Santa Fe Railroad and opened a clothing store in the small California desert town of Lucerne Valley and in 1956 he became a citizen. The man who killed Devil's Island lived quietly in his chosen home town. It had no excitement, but he had lived a life with enough excitement in it for 20 men. Perhaps, after all, what attracted him most to Lucerne Valley was that it was in the desert. Belbenoit, René, Prisoner Number 46,635, *Liberé* Number 36,444, had had enough of jungles.

THE LAST EXCURSION

AGED SEVENTY-TWO, not retired, and no current plans for retirement, "Fred J. Meyer," lives in Queens. He is willing enough to be quoted on any of a million subjects, but not on the one subject it is most likely that a writer would want to quote him. Few of his neighbors have any idea, in fact, that "Mr. Meyer" is one of the few survivors of one of the worst disasters that ever struck New York City—the death of the steamboat *General Slocum*. This was almost sixty years ago, but he hasn't forgotten it. He never will.

"I dream about it by night and I think about it by day," he says. "And I don't want a lot of people bothering me about it . . ."

The story of what happened to "Fred J. Meyer" that June day in 1904 is a true one, but that is not his true name, and some of the details in this chapter have been arranged to respect his privacy. Henceforth, the quotation marks around the name will be omitted.

Just as the boys of today want to be spacemen, the boys of his generation were steamboat-crazy. Fred says he "learned to read" by studying the names painted in large, ornate, curlicued Tuscan letters on the paddle-wheel boxes of the boats that were thick on the East River in those days—both freight and passenger vessels made regular runs, and from spring to fall there were the excursion boats. Admiral Dewey (whose maritime fame had been earned a long way from the East River) was a big figure to the boys, but not far behind him was "Captain Billy"—William Van Schaick, of the *General Slocum*. Some of the freight-steamers were dingy enough, but not Captain Billy's vessel. From May to

September her clean white silhouette glided up the river every morning and back every evening, sending the sounds of music and laughter floating across the water.

It had been fifty years since the *Henry Clay* had been wrecked off Riverdale. The resultant public clamor had resulted in the passing of the Steamboat Inspection Act. Racing was forbidden, boilers checked, and every craft carried a sufficient number of lifeboats, lifejackets, and lifesavers—at least in theory.

The trouble was, that the task of enforcing the Act was in the hands of a clutter of political appointees, worn-out hacks and wardheelers and almost to a man, Civil War veterans; still engaged in "driving a forty-mule-team through the Treasury"— and what they loaded on the wagon wasn't borax, either. There was nothing peculiar to the Steamboat Inspection Service in this. The President of the New York City Board of Aldermen, for instance, was a picturesque old crook named Dan Sickles, whose sole qualification for office was his left leg: it had been shot off at Gettysburg.

Fred knew nothing about all this. Nor did he know that Captain Van Schaick had one of the worst records afloat. A recent writer on the subject suggests, charitably, that he was "accident-prone," but no one in 1904 had ever heard the phrase. He was a veteran river-boatman, and all the river-boatmen stuck together. Billy was a mite clumsy at times, but he was a good fellow just the same. Still, they took good care to keep their distance when he was within bumping range . . .

The old German neighborhood in lower Manhattan, where Fred was raised, went from First Street up to Tenth, and from Third Avenue over to the East River. The inhabitants were hard-working, thrifty, church-going people, for the most part; and the leading parish in the district was St. Mark's Lutheran Church. It was the annual practice (as it still is for many churches near the New York waterways) for the parish to charter an excursion boat for a day, and sell tickets. This year the boat hired was the *General Slocum*, handsome and bewhiskered Captain Billy at the wheel; a band was engaged, beer laid on, and the destination was the popular picnic resort of Locust Grove, on Long Island's North Shore.

(As an aside—this writer's father, Harry J. Davidson, then a boy of twelve, had been invited to go along by friends, children of church members. Only a last-minute "premonition" of his mother's prevented him.)

That week in June Fred's father—a baker—was in between jobs. He'd left his place uptown to get one nearer home, on the promise of his wife's brother, Carl, also a baker. Tuesday afternoon Uncle Carl showed up while his sister was roasting the chickens and boiling the potatoes for the picnic lunch. She poured him coffee without bothering to ask. "Fred, I spoke to the boss," Carl said to his brother-in-law, "and he says you can come to start work tonight, if you want."

"Oh, not tonight," his sister pleaded. "Then he'll be too tired for the excursion tomorrow." Fred, Jr., added his pleas to hers. Every kid in the parish would have his mother with him, but few would be lucky enough to have a father along. Not on a weekday.

His father laughed. "You see, Carl? It's a plot between them."

"A night's work is a night's pay," said Uncle Carl, stolidly.

Mr. Meyer hesitated. Then he gave way. "Not tonight, tomorrow . . . No, tomorrow night I'll be coming back from Locust Grove too late. So—Thursday night without fail."

Uncle Carl shrugged, finished his coffee. Two night's work (and pay!) lost over a Sunday School picnic—well, he always thought his brother-in-law was frivolous. Imagine a sensible man marrying when he was only twenty! Shaking his head, he went out, leaving his sister still preparing the chickens, the potato salad, the sandwiches, eggs, radishes, pies, and cakes—she didn't allow her husband to bake at home! It took all three of them to carry that "little lunch" to the pier the next day.

It was Fred's opinion that at fourteen he was old enough to leave school and go to work. This was common, then; but it wasn't his parents' opinion, and he had to get permission to be excused from public school to attend the Sunday School outing. This wasn't difficult; the term was almost over, anyway.

They reached the Recreation Pier at the foot of Third Street a little before nine-thirty. Pastor Haas greeted them with his usual gentle smile. Pastor Schultz, his assistant, suggested that they'd better hurry. The best seats, he said, were almost all taken. The boat was due to leave, but no one hurried in those days, and the *Slocum* was held for stragglers till not long before ten o'clock. Fred heard people say that over 980 tickets had been sold, but these were all for those over twelve, those under traveled free. Then the band began to play Luther's hymn, *"Ein Feste Burg,"* the deck hands cast off the ropes, and the *General Slocum* started on her way, flags flying.

Fred had just gotten an idea, which he mentioned to his father: next summer he would apply for a summer-job as a deck hand. His father didn't think much of it. Deck hands, he said, had a bad name. Any riffraff willing to take the low wages offered was hired.

The boat had only gone a few miles, and was opposite Fifty-Seventh Street, when a boy prowling around below decks noticed a wisp of smoke coming from one of the cabins, and called it to the attention of a crew member named Cokely. Cokely told one of the stewards to take a look at it, and went to the bar for a glass of beer. The cabin held barrels containing either glasses or lamp-chimneys—the point was never made clear which, and is not important. What *was* important, though, is that the barrels were stuffed with straw or hay to prevent the glassware from breaking, in violation of the law prohibiting either hay or straw to be carried on passenger vessels. The steward must have been either drunk or half-witted, because his only act to deal with the smoke was to lay a bag of charcoal on the place the smoke was coming from—"to smother it," he said, later. Then he went away, confident that he had done all that could reasonably be expected of him.

The same boy presently came prowling back, observed that the smoke was still coming, and told another crew member. This time he was informed that what he had seen must have been steam. "This is a *steam* boat, remember, sonny?" People were always making that same mistake, the man said. They saw steam leaking from pipe-joints and got the idea that it was smoke.

Blackwell's Island (the present Welfare Island) slipped past, and then they were in the turbulent waters of Hell Gate. The whirling tide was rushing out to Long Island Sound, and dashing against the Mill Rocks. If any word or rumor of smoke reached Captain Van Shaick up above, he paid no attention to it. With his two copilot assistants he was holding the wheel steady as the ship trembled her way through the dangerous area.

"Let's go look at Astoria," Mr. Meyer suggested to his son. The women were chattering away happily, and the younger children were beginning to play, the first novelty of being water-borne having worn off. Father and son strolled over to the Astoria side and were looking at the boat-yards there when a dredge blew its whistle—and then blew it again—and then, very quickly, twice more. A man leaned out and gestured at the *Slocum*, pointing. In a moment he was behind, dwindling in the distance. Mr. Meyer took a firm grip on the railing and leaned far out. Fred copied him. Just forward of the *Slocum's* smokestacks, but on a lower deck, they saw a white puff of something—

"Smoke, Papa?"

"*Nein, dampf.*" But he didn't seem sure it *was* steam. While he gazed, uncertainly, they heard other boats and ships begin to sound their whistles. The passengers began to look up, but the noise only pleased them, they thought the whistles were greeting, and many waved their handkerchiefs.

Every fire on shipboard is serious, but the position of the *Slocum* and her passengers was not yet critical. Captain Van Schaick knew those waters intimately, and many choices were available to him. For one thing, he could have berthed his vessel at any of the many boat-yards in Astoria. Failing that, he could run her aground on the Sunken Meadows, as had the skipper of the *Seawanhake*, some years before, when that boat had caught afire, and unloaded his passengers onto the other craft with which the river was aswarm. Or he could veer over and dock at the Hundred and Thirtieth Street wharves, or even further up at the Health Department Pier in the Bronx.

And if none of these alternatives had occurred to him or to his copilots, if they had lost their wits completely, if he had simply stopped dead in mid-channel, then, even though there might have been some loss of life through panic, most of those aboard could have been saved by the other boats in the river.

But Van Schaick did none of these things. He blundered, as he had blundered so often before, and this blunder was to be his last.

Mr. Meyer told Fred to find his mother and to stay with her, while he went to look for the First Mate, Flanagan, whom he had seen only a moment before. Mrs. Meyer was talking with a friend from the church, Mrs. Heintz, and some other women, one of whom held up her hand for silence. "Why are so many whistles blowing?" she asked. "Look—" She pointed to a factory where white puffs of steam were followed by as many tooting noises.

By this time fire alarms were being pulled all over upper Manhattan and Astoria. Every one was responded to, and in each case the result was the same: the engines came down to the water's edge, horses at the gallop, only to observe the *General Slocum* go right on by, smoke pouring from her lower deck, without once coming in close enough to shore for any fire engine to reach her. From her berth lower down the river, the fireboat *Zophar Mills* started in pursuit, sounding her siren. She was fast, but the *Slocum* had a huge head start, and never slackened speed for a second.

Fred Meyer, Sr., had no difficulty finding First Mate Flanagan. He was over on the port side of the afterdeck directing a group of crewmen who were uncoiling the hose from its place on the bulkhead. Noticing the startled looks produced by this activity, the elder Meyer acted quickly to forestall panic. "Don't get in the way of the crew while they are holding fire drill," he said, in German—emphasizing *drill*.

Germans are obedient people, and everybody withdrew to give the crew room. If it had really been a drill, it would have been the first held aboard the *Slocum* within memory—despite the law requiring it to be held regularly. Sweating and cursing, the crew struggled to straighten the kinks out of the hose, which hadn't been uncoiled since it was first wound on. A dribble of water came from the nozzle—then a strong flow—then the hose seemed to crack open in a dozen places and the water spurted from the leaks.

Young Fred heard one woman comment, "It is a bad hose," in the disapproving tone of a housewife who had seen roaches in someone else's kitchen.

Moving fast, the deck hands disappeared. Looking up, those on the afterdeck became aware that the crowd had increased. More and more people were coming from the forward deck. Fred heard bits of conversation. "*Ich weiss nicht*—the policeman said we had to move back here." "The fire drill?" *Also*: "the fire drill, *ja*." And they called to their children.

Above the murmur of talk the voice of Patrolman Van Tassel, one of the two policemen required on every excursion boat was heard calling, "Move on back, please," like a horsecar conductor. "Move on—back—"

Ahead of the *Slocum* a tug began to sound its whistle. The flames eating up the lower deck were horribly visible to those on the river. The *Slocum* didn't pause, but the tug did. As two men desperately cast loose the lines fastening it to its tow, a schooner, its skipper turned around to pursue the burning boat whose own skipper seemed deaf—if not dead.

Now Patrolman Kelk had come back, herding the increasingly nervous passengers who hadn't heeded Van Tassel's orders. "No, you can't go this way. *Move on back, please. Keep moving*!" The sweat was dripping down his red face, gathering in beads in his long mustache. "*Get back, get back, get back—*"

The fire was forward, but the speed of the boat, racing up a wind, was driving it aft. And still most of the passengers had no idea that the boat was on fire at all!

By now it seemed that all the craft on the East River were pursuing the ship, as men might pursue a madman. The air was a frenzied blast of noise from their whistles—and then this was drowned out by a sudden chorus of shouts and cries from below. The passengers below on the hurricane deck had just discovered the fire. They had not yet discovered—as they soon would—that they were caught, that there was no escape—except the river.

There was a sudden pause, slight and brief, such as occurs in every rage of noise, and in that second those who recognized the one sound which didn't stop felt their flesh turn to ice as they heard through the short quiet the crackling of the flames. And then, behind, very far behind, the hoarse, harsh siren of the fireboat *Zophar Mills*. It was wailing demoniacally. Those who turned their heads could see her racing in pursuit.

The Meyers, by unspoken consent, kept together. Even when the fire ripped out into open sight and its noise grew to a roar, they kept together. Suddenly a man clutched at Mr. Meyer's sleeve. It was Pastor Haas. He gasped one word—*"Lifeboats!"*

The Meyers, father and son, rushed after him. A cabin door burst open and two crewmen appeared, lifebelts flapping around them. At once women and children ran to them, asking for help in finding the other lifebelts. The reply was brief. One crewman knocked down the woman in front of him, the other dodged around. Then the two of them hurtled the railing and jumped overboard. Neither had bothered with the lifeboats. The minister and Fred and his father soon learned why. *The lifeboats were fastened to the decks with wire cable and were absolutely immovable!*

Pastor Haas rushed off to find his wife. All around, screaming women groped, coughing through the smoke and burning embers, crying out for their children, as Fred and his father made their way back to the afterdeck.

When his father saw them leaping, vainly, for lifebelts fastened overhead, his self-control, for the first time, snapped. He bellowed with rage, picked up a chair and smashed it to pieces. Then, with one of the legs, he began to pry loose the precious jackets from their wire fastenings. The first one he seized tore apart in his hands, the rotten canvas releasing a shower of sawdust . . .

A lone rowboat now put alongside the *Slocum*, and the man at the oars shouted for people to jump. In an instant the tiny boat was filled and about to push off when a crewman was seen letting himself over the railing. "No more now," the oarsman cried. "I'll come back—no more now—" But the crewman jumped, fell crashing into the little craft, capsizing it. Everyone was tossed into the river.

One man, thinking only of escape, began to batter his fists upon a door, without considering where it might lead. In a moment a crowd was beside and behind him, all doing the same thing. The door gave. It led only to the huge paddle wheel, now turning and churning at top speed. Before those in front could turn back, those in back had thrust forward, pressing the first ones into the flashing spokes.

For them, at least, death came quickly.

A boat left its dock as the *Slocum* swept by, and came toward her, whistle blowing, as if to invite her to berth there. People swept toward the rail on that side. A man in oily dungarees tried to force his way through the frenzied crowd, but they only pressed tighter together. He raised his arm—a huge wrench was in his hand, and he brought it down again and again on the heads, arms, and shoulders of the fear-crazed women. Rushing forward over the bloody path he had cleared for himself, he poised at the rail, prepared to leap.

There was a noise like an explosion. Part of the deck seemed to leap into the air. Flames jumped higher than the top of the superstructure—and then even that part of the superstructure itself gave way and plunged down into the heart of the blaze. For one awful second it seemed as if the man stood poised on the burning rail, his clothes blazing, his mouth still open and shrieking wordlessly—then he vanished into the glowing, roaring pit.

The smell of burning hair and clothes, the odor of burning flesh, hit the faces of the passengers like a blast from the fires of Hell.

Then a woman cried out, screaming, pointing into the racing water itself. A little girl was in the water, her arms reaching upward, blood coursing down her terror-stricken face. Almost at once she was swept astern. Two more children bobbed past. The woman let out a long and terrible scream.

"Frieda! Frieda! I'm coming!"

Before anyone could stop her, she had reached the rail and jumped.

Kelk, the policeman, his tall helmet discarded and forgotten, seemed to sense what was coming. He faced the terrified crowd, arms spread wide. *"No!"* he cried. *"No—No—"* But his words were lost. At that moment panic swept the crowd. All control was lost. Shouts of fright drowned out his voice. In a single second everyone began to run. And at the same instant a hot and choking blast of smoke billowed up amidships, and a woman darted aft, screaming, her hair and dress a mass of flames.

The whistle of the *General Slocum* began now, for no reason then or since discernible by human reason, to shriek. Someone was still in the wheelhouse, and had evidently decided that the ship was in need of help . . .

By ones and twos, then by dozens, then—too fast for the eye to register the number—the passengers began to jump over the side of the ship.

There was a niche in the bulkhead at one place, where a water-barrel had been. A woman crouched there now, an odd little smile on her face. Unattended by any of the few who noticed her, numbed with horror, she gave birth to a child. She ripped off part of her petticoat and wrapped it around the tiny form. Then she got to her feet, pushing against the bulkhead with one hand, walked slowly to the rail through the smoke and screams, the half-smile never leaving her face. Then she threw herself into the swirling waters.

The wake of the *General Slocum* wasn't marked with foam. It was marked with heads of those who preferred the mercy of the river to the mercy of the flames. They bobbed up and down like jetsam. And then, while those still aboard watched and screamed, they vanished, one by one.

Only at one place aboard was there still a trace of order. A tug had come alongside, and, while Officer Van Tassel helped maintain the crowd in some semblance of control, his partner, Kelk, was taking the baby children their mothers handed to him, and dropped them into the waiting arms of the men in the tug below. But time was running out. The Meyer family—father, mother, and son—were at the rail, waiting their chance to jump into or as near to the tug as they could. There was another puff of flame, billowing out onto those remaining, a red cloud with yellow stars burning in it; and with this came the last and most awful panic of all those which Fred Meyer remembers. His hands parted from his parents'. Feet trampled him. Then railing and deck gave way together, and the water of the East River hit him on the side like a blow from a club.

His eyes caught one picture just before he went under—a picture which has haunted his days and nights for fifty-eight years: the white petticoats of the women and girls fluttering in the air as they leaped and fell into the rushing waters; and the *General Slocum*, flames enveloping her from bow to stern, her whistle still screaming insanely as she fled up the river to her doom . . .

Fred learned later that the boat which pulled him out of the water, half-conscious, was the Department of Correction vessel *Massasoit*. Captain Parkinson heard the clamor as it rose from every ship, boat, dock, and factory whistle in upper Manhattan, the south Bronx, and east Queens. He could see the smoke and fire rising higher than the *Slocum's* stacks as she headed toward Long Island Sound. It made no sense, but he guessed (and correctly) that she was heading for North Brother Island, a dot of land used for city hospitals; but he didn't know which channel she would try to make. As soon as he saw her round the point of North Brother and aim straight for shore, he headed for her at full speed. Without slackening pace his boat snatched up several survivors, including young Meyer.

Insofar as Captain Van Schaick had had any plan at all, this seems to have been it: to beach his vessel on the small strip of sand on one side of North Brother Island. For this he had passed up any number of nearer and better places, and with this almost within sight he gave it up—no one knew why, or has ever learned why—and rammed her into the shallows twenty-five feet from the little island's sea wall.

The *Massasoit* drew so much water she couldn't get within fifty feet of the blazing wreck. Captain Parkinson shouted, "Boats—the boats—" But the crew didn't move fast enough for the coxswain, a huge redhead named Jake Rappaport. He was first in the water, and passed the *Massasoit's* boats on his way back with two babies he'd fished from the river.

There were still people alive on the *Slocum*, and they were still screaming. The nurses and T.B. patients from the hospital on the island formed a chain of bodies into the water up to their necks. Captain Ben Wade lashed his dirty little tug fast to the blazing ship and used it as a bridge to the Health Department boat *Edson*, until the *Wade* itself began to burn, and the tug *Goldenrod* took its place.

The *Zophar Mills*, her sirens no longer screaming, at last caught up, and played her hoses on the burning *Slocum* and her rescuers. The waters were full of people—but most of them seemed to be floating face down.

Fred Meyer found himself in the *Massasoit's* small boat, this time with coxswain Jake Rappaport. He scanned every face, but didn't see his parents. A Negro named Sam Patchen, in a yawl, saved the last batch of *Slocum* survivors from the box of the paddle wheel. The hair was scorched from their heads.

Suddenly, everyone—and everyone had been looking down into the river—looked up.

There was a boy on the flagpole.

Fred recognized him by sight, but neither then nor afterward has he been able to recall his name. A blond, curly-headed kid. They shouted to him, but there was no way to reach him. He was showing no fright; as the flames licked at him, he climbed higher. Then one great moan went up from the watching throng ashore and in the boats. The pole shivered—staggered—the boy never made a single sound—and the pole fell forward into the fire.

That ended the rescue of the living. The rescue of the dead went on.

They wouldn't let Fred go back into the boats. "Can't you stand to look at the bodies?" a nurse asked him. "If you can, if you know any of them, tell us, and we'll write the name on a tag."

He said that he could stand it, but asked them first to take his own name, so that his parents would know he was alive. Not till he said, "My father is a powerful swimmer," did the nurse realize that they, too, had been on the *Slocum*. She gave him a pitying look, but she took his name.

First the shore was lined with bodies. Then the lawn of the city hospital on North Brother Island was filled. Then they filled the doctor's quarters, the halls, the stables—the dead were everywhere. The rescued passengers who could walk stumbled down the rows of bodies. Women screamed hysterically as they recognized their children. A hundred policemen were ferried in, and went out in the water, wading and grappling.

"What is this in the women's hair?" a nurse asked another, in a low voice. Fred looked. The loose, tangled hair was clotted with a brown and powdery substance. "It's sawdust," he said. There was a life belt on the body of the woman. Automatically, he said, "This is Mrs. Reiner." A helper wrote the name on a tag, tied it to the cold, wet wrist. "The life belts were filled with sawdust . . ."

Two policemen stripped to their vests staggered up just then, another body on the stretcher. "Why *sawdust?*" the nurse asked, confused.

"The bastards!" one of the policemen swore. "Sorry, ladies— sawdust? The life belts were supposed to have cork in them, slabs of it—these have cork in them, all right—cork sawdust! No damn good at all—" he reached over and ripped at the canvas cover with his fingernails. It split instantly, and the sodden, powdery cork dust oozed out. "Waterlogged!" he spit the word out. "The dirty bastards who made it—the filthy bastards who sold it—the lousy bastards who bought it! Sorry, ladies—sorry." Tears poured down his cheeks.

"Them is dummies," said his partner. "Good to fool the inspectors. Ye might as well jump overboard with so much lead strapped to yez. Go down like a rock . . ."

Hour after hour Fred scanned the faces of the dead, naming them when he could. Then someone took him to the kitchens, fed him, gave him coffee—strong and hot. Then he was out with the dead again. "This is Mrs. Timms . . . This is Mrs. Heintz . . . This is Lena Ackerman . . ." By ten at night there were over four hundred bodies tagged, and there was no more room, unless the dead crowded out the living. So the work of moving the bodies to the Bellevue morgue began. Fred went along. No one questioned his right to do so.

There was a vast crowd gathered at the hospital as the bodies began to arrive. Moans and sobs went up. One policeman said to another, "We haven't the half of them yet." He was right. "There won't be enough coffins on Manhattan Island for to bury them all." He was right.

Fred remembers a confused, weird scene. A line of men bending with the weight of the stretchers bearing the dead. A throng of people sobbing and wailing in the half-lit darkness; gas-jets flaring. The shuffle of feet. Suddenly a door opens and a group of men come out. One has his face heavily bandaged—not that his curly moustache and sandy side whiskers cannot be seen, though—a man on the small side. A policeman holding him firmly by each arm. All three seem to look up at the same moment. The man in the middle takes in the scene, cries out, tries to cover his eyes. A policeman says, "Don't take him through here!" They turn and go back, stumbling . . .

Fred has recognized the man in the middle, but is so overwhelmed by a rush of emotions that he says nothing. It is Captain Van Schaick. The law which allowed him for so many years to run free in his blundering way with his firetrap ship now has him firmly in hand.

The nightmare begins again—the dead bodies, the dead faces. "This is George Heintz—" His brother Peter stands by, waiting for someone to take him and his dead away. His mother, his brother, his sister, his aunt—he can't explain how he was saved —the terror and tragedy have deprived him of voice. Peter cannot speak a word. He is twelve years old. "This is Mrs. Burfiend— Mrs. Ebeling—"

Their husbands are present, they come forward, unwilling and unbelieving: the shock of recognition drives them out of their minds; hospital helpers lead the shrieking men away. A relative of the Rheinfrank family screams hysterically, "Eleven dead! Eleven dead!" A man is caught trying to steal Mrs. Fisher's purse and is rescued from the half-mad crowd by police. Mrs. Fischer alone says nothing. Her eyes stare glassily upward. *The dead praise not the Lord . . .*

Fred Meyer next remembers driving through the dark streets of lower Manhattan. His Uncle Carl is at the reins of the wagons he had hired to bring the bodies back to the undertakers. There were no more hearses to be had on the whole island. The horse's hooves went clopping on the stone blocks of the street. They passed another wagon, the driver hunched over, in front. In back, a woman, with a familiar face. The woman was dead, wrapped in a sheet, pillows propping her up. It was her husband driving.

At the Department of Charities' Morgue the same scenes were being repeated as at Bellevue. The morgue pier, whence dead paupers were removed to the Potter's Field, was crowded with the *General Slocum's* dead, there being no room for all of them in one place. Uncle and nephew scanned the faces of the victims, but the ones they sought were not there. Finally, exhausted, they went home to sleep.

While they were in bed the sleepless quest continued on the East River, whose heedless waters slowly swept their unsought burdens up and down the shores. In the shallows, lanterns on poles lit up the water for the searchers. The police-boat Patrol played its searchlight farther out, and gas-flares on barges aided the work. But not all who were aboard that night desired bright light. Ghouls, their faces blackened with charcoal, prowled in boats with muffled oars. When swollen fingers refused to surrender engagement or wedding rings to the grasp of the thieves, a slash of a knife did the work; even ears were cut off . . .

By morning over eight hundred bodies had been recovered, but not that of Mr. and Mrs. Meyer. The authorities blasted the river with dynamite, and scores of bodies rose—shattered by the explosion. And meanwhile, steamboat after steamboat went on past the grisly scene, bands playing, flags flying—just as the *Slocum* had done only the day before—people dancing, or gaping over the railing. Two flatboats were floated over with field artillery pieces on board them. Coroner O'Gorman, a stout and florid man with the long mustache of the day, ordered the excursion boats to sheer off.

"The water is free!" one captain shouted; derisively adding, "So don't spoil the show!"

O'Gorman's face turned the color of liver. "Lieutenant," he turned to the officer in charge of the artillery, "can you reach that vessel with your cannons?"

"Yes, and blow the son-of-a-bitch out of his pilot-house!" the lieutenant shouted.

The excursion boat swiftly fled the scene. The guns began to boom. It was like shaking a tree in reverse. Up the bodies came —eleven—another salvo—sixteen bodies—the guns boomed— twelve bodies. While the artillery rested, divers went down, groping in the murk and mud for any bodies not dislodged yet. They found some. This new harvest was put aboard the *Massasoit*. The coffins were piled tier on tier from bow to stern; as soon as they were unloaded, the bodies were taken from the dark red charity coffins and placed on stretchers and the empty boxes sent back for another load.

Among those taken from the river that morning were Fred's parents, clasped in each other's arms.

There were still no coffins to be had. There were still no hearses. In from the other boroughs they finally came—but the undertakers had no room. Embalmers were imported from Long Island. Every house on Sixth Street, it seemed, was hung with black crepe in the doorway for a dead adult, and with white flowers for a dead child. Between Grand Street and Tenth Street the two mourners tramped to fifteen undertakers before they found one who could take their dead. But they had to lie on the sidewalk in hastily improvised boxes till there was room inside.

Crowds gathered to gawk and gossip. "President Roosevelt sent $500." "So did Cardinal Farley." "—the President of France —" "—the Mayor of Glasgow—"

Inside, a woman was screaming hysterically in front of two tiny coffins and a standard-sized one. "You didn't want to go, mother, did you? But I made you! I killed you! I thought you'd have a fine day's outing, but now you're dead, and the babies are dead, too!" Then, crying wildly, *"I'm coming! I'm coming!"* she dashed out into the street and tried to throw herself under a horsecar. They dragged her away.

A hundred German-speaking policemen toured the parish, asking people to come and examine the great piles of children's straw hats, the parasols, gocarts, handbags, the baby-carriages. By now it was obvious that dozens of bodies were too badly burned to be ever identified for certain. The little sister of the Heintz family had been missing; her body wasn't with the others. Two days later she was washed ashore at the Clinton Street pier—only a block from her home.

One hundred and five grave-diggers were at work in the Lutheran cemetery in Middle Village, Queens. For the sixty-one unknown dead they dug what came to be known as The Great Grave. Cardinal Farley ordered the bells of all Roman Catholic churches to be tolled along with those of the Protestant churches when that great procession of hearses passed through on its solemn journey. The Meyers' funeral was on Friday. From earliest morning until sundown what seemed like a continuous line of hearses and funeral carriages passed across the Williamsburg Bridge. Every Lutheran minister for miles around was pressed into service. There was no music—St. Mark's choir had been wiped out. A brief prayer—a psalm—that was all. White and black hearses. White and black carriages.

Over one thousand dead, mostly women and children.

Coroners O'Gorman and Berry began their preliminary hearing on Monday. Ex-Fire Marshal Freel was assigned to make an investigation of the wreck, which lay on the mud on her port side in eighteen feet of water. District Attorney William Travers Jerome (he had a cousin who was beginning to be well-known as a journalist and budding politician, by the name of Winston Churchill), and his assistant, Gavan, were present to hear the evidence. It was reported that President Theodore Roosevelt had already dismissed eight inspectors and two supervisors from the Steamboat Inspection Service.

Coroner O'Gorman said that "the crew made no effort to save the passengers. *The crew were guilty of the worst cowardice imaginable.* They made no attempt to use the hose on the other side of the ship." Freel reported that one of the fire-cocks had been blocked with a rubber plug—that the hose which split had no rubber lining and had been bought for sixteen cents a foot, when Fire Department hose cost over a dollar a foot!

Coroner O'Gorman went on to say, "The failure of the crew to aid the passengers was appalling. *Only one member of the crew died...*"

Fire Marshal Freel reported seven barrels of hay or straw in the *General Slocum's* "second cabin," where the fire started, although the law forbade either commodity to be carried on a passenger vessel. He added that the cabin was also stored with paint, kerosene, and other inflammables.

The damning testimony continued to unfold. The fire had been known to crew members for over fifty blocks before anyone reported it to the chief engineer! The chief's duty was to turn on the water for the hoses and to flood the cabin with steam to smother the fire.

Coroner Berry: Did you turn on the steam?

Chief Engineer Conklin: I couldn't—there was no steam pipe

in that cabin!

Coroner Berry: Was the chief at his post when the fire started?

Second Mate Corcoran: No, he wasn't.

Coroner Berry: How long did he remain at his post after learning of the fire?

Second Mate Corcoran: He jumped into the first tug that came along, and he was the first to jump.

Coroner Berry: How many fire drills a week are required by law?

First Mate Flanagan: Three, I think. Three.

Coroner: Don't know? How long have you been licensed?

First Mate: I haven't got no license.

Coroner: Well, how many fire drills did you hold this season?

First Mate: None, I think.

O'Gorman said, "There was floating cork dust an inch deep on the water. Some of the life belts were stuffed with dried reeds." Former Fire Marshal Freel said that the law required solid cork. The belts were stamped, *PASSED U. S. ASS'T. INSPECTOR of Steam Vessels N. Y. Jun. 18, 1891*. "These life belts are thirteen years old," he said.

O'Gorman: What is the life span of a life belt?

Freel: No more than eight years—if it was good to start with.

O'Gorman: Was this one from the *Slocum*—it is from the *Slocum*?

Freel: From the *General Slocum*, yes sir.

O'Gorman: Was it good to start with?

Freel: It was worthless to start with.

Inspector Lundgren, who'd given the *Slocum* a clean bill of health only a few weeks before, was called to the stand. He refused to testify. It was the first time anyone in those days could recall that a government employee had invoked the Fifth Amendment.

A Mr. Barnaby, said to be the dead vessel's owner, declared that he had spent money on new life belts. "I have the bills to prove it," he said. The bills were presented.

Berry examined them, scowled, held them up to the light, "These have been altered! They were originally made out to the *Great Republic*. You own her, too, don't you?"

Barnaby said, "Oh, I personally own neither. They belong to the Knickerbocker Navigation Company—I am merely a stockholder." The largest stockholder? Yes. And the president? Yes. Drawing a salary of—? Ten thousand a year. Did you visit the *Slocum* this season to see if everything was in order? Oh, said Barnaby, he was "merely a businessman. I leave those details to Captain Pease of the *Grand Republic*. He's a stockholder, too."

Captain Pease was old and deaf. Had he been aboard the *Slocum* this season? Hey? What's that? Oh. No. Certainly not. He left that to Captain Van Schaick. Captain Van Schaick said that he left it to First Mate Flanagan (unlicensed). First Mate Flanagan said that *he* left it to Inspector Lundberg.

And what did Lundberg have to say?

"I decline to answer on the grounds that it might tend to incriminate or degrade me."

Coroner O'Gorman: When is the Knickerbocker Navigation Company going to raise the wreck to see if there are still bodies trapped aboard?"

Barnaby: It's not up to us—the hulk belongs to the insurance company now.

The insurance company said that it couldn't spend more than $5,000 to raise her. And the wrecking company, whose divers were still at work, said it would cost a lot more than that. This was the signal for old General Dan Sickles to get into the act. Waving his crutch at the newspaper reporters whom he had called into his office, he declared that he had wired the President of the United States for an investigation; and that he was calling the Board of Aldermen into session to appropriate enough money to raise the wreck. $25,000 was the sum allocated, peanuts to the general, who, ten years later, when in his nineties, was accused of having filched $90,000 from the Gettysburg Battlefield Fund, at which he was Custodian.

As a result of the investigation, Captain Van Schaick was tried for "misconduct, negligence, and inattention to duty as master of his vessel." Why hadn't he held any fire drills, he was asked. He said that he had—but couldn't remember when. Why hadn't he put the *Slocum* ashore at Astoria? He said that he didn't know she was afire! Well, why hadn't he run her aground on the Sunken Meadow bank? The current was too strong. And his reason for not having taken her in to the Hundred and Thirtieth Street Dock? A tug had warned him off—he might have set fire to the coal yards there! Then why hadn't he brought her to the Health Department dock in the Bronx? The current, again, was too strong. It was flood tide, too.

"I put her on the nearest place possible," he protested. "Not one captain in fifty would've remembered that little piece of land where I beached her, else she'd surely have split on the rocks, the boilers would've busted, and the whole lot been killed by steam . . . You're making me the scapegoat!" he cried. Then he buried his face in his seared hands and wept.

The jury was out only ten minutes. The verdict was Guilty. Captain Van Schaick was sentenced to ten years, of which he served three and a half, working in the greenhouse in Sing Sing. When he came out he married a nurse, rather long in the tooth, who had fallen in love with him while tending to his burns. They settled in upstate New York. Captain Billy kept insisting that he was willing to return to the river at the drop of a hat, that he "knew everything there was to know about steamboating," but —somehow—nobody seemed to listen.

The hulk of the *General Slocum* was finally raised, and sold for $1,800. As the liability of the Knickerbocker Navigation Company was limited to the value of the "bottom," each bereaved family was legally entitled to sue for a share of this, which came to about a dollar and a half per family—those families of which there were still survivors, that is: some were entirely wiped out. The Knickerbocker line was forced out of business, too.

The hulk was converted into a barge and spent the rest of

its career hauling coal. There were dark mutterings of a "curse" when, first one and then another of the barge personnel were killed by falling off the craft, which finally sank off the Jersey coast during the First World War.

And the survivors? There were over a thousand dead. There were people scarred and crippled for life. Some had gone insane. Hundreds of children were orphaned. A society was organized, the *Vereinigung der General Slocum Hinterbliebenen*, the Organization of the *General Slocum* Survivors. It held—and still holds, though their number has naturally dwindled over the years—annual memorial services at the Middle Village Cemetery, where a monument shows a ship burning in the water. But this was to come later. At the time, the Organization's president, Charles Desch, said its purpose was to see "that other homes shall not be destroyed as ours have been." The purpose was successful. The laws were revised and enforced; there has never been another excursion-boat horror comparable to the one that turned fourteen-year-old Fred Meyer into a man with dreadful memories to last the rest of his life.

ABOUT THE AUTHOR

Avram Davidson (1923 – 1993)

Avram Davidson was born in New York in 1923 and was active in SF fandom from his teens. He is remembered as a writer of fantasy fiction, science fiction and crime fiction, as well as many stories that defy easy categorization. Among his SF and Fantasy awards are two Hugos, two World Fantasy Awards and a World Fantasy Life Achievement award; he also won a Queen's Award and an Edgar Award in the mystery genre. Although best known for his writing, Davidson also edited *The Magazine of Fantasy and Science Fiction* from 1962 to 1964. He died in 1993.

ALSO BY AVRAM DAVIDSON

Vergil Magus

1. *The Phoenix and the Mirror (1966)*
2. *Vergil in Averno (1986)*
3. *The Scarlet Fig: Or Slowly Through a Land of Stone (2005)*

Kar-Chee

4. *The Kar-Chee Reign (1966)*
5. *Rogue Dragon (1966)*

Peregrine

6. *Peregrine: Primus (1971)*
7. *Peregrine: Secundus (1975)*
8. *Peregrine Parentus* and Other Tales *(with Ethan Davidson) (2016)*

Other Novels

9. *Joyleg (with Ward Moore)*

10. *Mutiny in Space* (1964)
11. *Rork! (1965)*
12. *Masters of the Maze (1965)*
13. *Clash of the Star-Kings (1966)*
14. *The Enemy of My Enemy (1966)*
15. *The Island Under the Earth (1969)*
16. *Ursus of Ultima Thule (1973)*
17. *The Adventures of Doctor Eszterhazy (1969)*
18. *Marco Polo and the Sleeping Beauty (with Grania Davis) (1988)*
19. *The Boss in the Wall: A Treatise on the House Devil (with Grania Davis) (1998)*
20. *Beer! Beer! Beer!(2021)*
21. *Dragons In The Trees (2022)*

Collections

22. *Or All the Seas with Oysters* (1962)
23. *Crimes & Chaos (1962)*
24. *What Strange Stars and Skies (1965)*
25. *Strange Seas and Shores* (1971)
26. *The Enquiries of Doctor Eszterhazy (1975)*
27. *The Redward Edward Papers* (1978)
28. *Avram Davidson: Collected Fantasies (1982)*
29. *The Avram Davidson Treasury* (1990)
30. *The Adventures of Doctor Eszterhazy* (1991)
31. *Adventures in Unhistory: Conjectures on the Factual Foundations of Several Ancient Legends* (1991)
32. *The Investigations of Avram Davidson (1999)*
33. *The Other Nineteenth Century (2001)*
34. *Everybody Has Somebody in Heavan (2000)*
35. *Limekiller! (2003)*
36. *Skinny* – A short Story (2021)
37. Avram Davidson turns 100 title TBD (2023)

www.ingramcontent.com/pod-product-compliance
Lightning Source LLC
Chambersburg PA
CBHW022105280326
41933CB00007B/263